Partners in Mission

Anglican Consultative Council
Second Meeting
DUBLIN IRELAND
17–27 July 1973

LONDON **SPCK** 1973

First published in 1973
by SPCK
Holy Trinity Church
Marylebone Road
London NW1 4DU

Printed in Great Britain by
Eyre & Spottiswoode Ltd, Thanet Press, Margate

SBN 281 02774 9

CONTENTS

The Council is to enable Anglicans to 'fulfil their common inter-Anglican and ecumenical responsibilities in promoting the unity, renewal, and mission of Christ's Church'.   (*The Lambeth Conference 1968*, p. 145)

TERMS OF REFERENCE

Resolution 69 of the Lambeth Conference 1968 assigned to the Anglican Consultative Council these functions:

1 To share information about developments in one or more provinces with the other parts of the communion and to serve as needed as an instrument of common action.

2 To advise on inter-Anglican, provincial, and diocesan relationships, including the division of provinces, the formation of new provinces and of regional councils, and the problems of extra-provincial dioceses.

3 To develop as far as possible agreed Anglican policies in the world mission of the Church and to encourage national and regional Churches to engage together in developing and implementing such policies by sharing their resources of manpower, money, and experience to the best advantage of all.

4 To keep before national and regional Churches the importance of the fullest possible Anglican collaboration with other Christian Churches.

5 To encourage and guide Anglican participation in the Ecumenical Movement and the ecumenical organizations; to co-operate with the World Council of Churches and the world confessional bodies on behalf of the Anglican Communion; and to make arrangements for the conduct of pan-Anglican conversations with the Roman Catholic Church, the Orthodox Churches, and other Churches.

6 To advise on matters arising out of national or regional church union negotiations or conversations and on subsequent relations with united Churches.

7 To advise on problems of inter-Anglican communication and to help in the dissemination of Anglican and ecumenical information.

8 To keep in review the needs that may arise for further study and, where necessary, to promote inquiry and research.

ABBREVIATIONS

ACC	Anglican Consultative Council
ARCIC	Anglican–Roman Catholic International Commission
CASA	Consejo Anglicano Sud Americano (Anglican Council for South America)
CPSA	Church of the Province of South Africa
CSI	Church of South India
ICET	International Consultation on English Texts
LCR	Lambeth Conference Resolution
MRI	Mutual Responsibility and Interdependence in the Body of Christ
WCC	World Council of Churches
Limuru	refers to the Report, entitled *The Time is Now*, of the First Meeting of the Anglican Consultative Council, 1971

PREFACE

The second meeting of the Anglican Consultative Council took place in a peaceful Dublin, but under constantly cloudy skies, intended, as it seemed, to keep us in mind that there is being worked out in this small island a tragedy and a judgement of the western world.

As at Limuru, Kenya, in 1971, the Council was a meeting of Anglicans gathered from all quarters of the world, chosen as representatives by their home Churches. Journeys that ended in Dublin began in thirty-four different countries. Nearly two-thirds of the members were the same as at Limuru, but this meeting was markedly, though elusively, different from Limuru.

Probably the essential difference was simply that Limuru was a first meeting, Dublin the second. Limuru experienced, with the impact of personal discovery, the family unity in Christ of the world's nationalities, races, and cultures. Dublin resumed, but also assumed, all that, and was able to begin feeling out the differences in our Christian experiences, thinking, and hopes. This was a little more mature, a little less easy, a little less immediately productive, a little less apparently adventurous. But if the deeper understanding of one another's perspectives and aspirations that began to be sketched into the Council's character can be more fully drawn in the coming years, then the Council will be valuable indeed.

This development towards the Council's understanding of itself had several effects. The touch of uncertainty meant that at times there was resort to the style of a conventional synod with less of the sparkle that had been refreshing at Limuru. Of more lasting importance was an emerging discussion about theology. Some members thought that, even with the important contribution of the consultants, there was too small a theological voice. Others thought that theology was too highly exalted at the expense of the insights which spring from contemporary Christian experience. Significantly, from another angle, the adequacy and relevance of traditional theological method, and its ability to comprehend Christian theology of other styles, was challenged. In another direction, the Council recognized again that while voices of youth need to be heard, the problem often is to begin to understand what the voice is saying, and why.

So the differences and discontinuities within the Council are beginning to be detected. Were they to remain hidden the Council should not hope to approach its potential. If, however, they can be understood and appreciated, there is some rich, but yet unknown, harvest ahead.

Such are some first brief reflections of one person on the background of this Report of the second meeting of the Council. The text of the

Report must speak for itself. The word 'partners' in the title refers more to Christian aspiration than to Christian accomplishment. Partnership is a basic theme running through the work of each Section of the Council: partnership with Christ—in his divided Church, in a world of unjust human relationships, in ministry, in activity within the Anglican Communion. In every case the imperfect partnership needs to be advanced towards perfection—in every case for the mission of Christ. The title *Partners in Mission* is perhaps more apt and less glib than a passing glance might indicate.

Readers of this Report may feel that the Council needlessly reiterates (e.g. in Section 3) that its function is to consult, not to legislate; to advise not to direct. But it may be well that the Council makes plain its understanding of the role and place it has in the tradition of Anglican family life. The family confers together in responsible consultation; then, aware of the consultation, each member Church makes such decisions for itself as seem right in its circumstance. A useful expression of the underlying principle was given in 1908 in the Encyclical Letter of the Lambeth Conference of that year:

If the Anglican Communion is to render that service to the varied needs of mankind to which the Church of our day is specially called, regard must be had both to the just freedom of its several parts, and to the just claims of the whole Communion upon its every part.

In Dublin the reports presented by the four sections came in turn before the full Council, were amended and finally received by it. They are now the reports and resolutions of the Council. However, there has been no attempt to impose a uniform style, or even to make them inhumanly consistent at every point.

Voting was by a show of hands. Whenever a count was asked for it has been recorded in the Report, and individual votes or abstentions recorded if the member concerned asked for it. Other votes were either unanimous or nearly so, with the exception of Resolution 26, where there was a substantial minority vote. The point at issue was whether a simpler resolution to the same effect would have been preferable.

With the exception of the six co-opted members, who are nominated by the Council, the people voting on all the issues and debating them were appointed to membership by their own Churches. They did not choose themselves, for the ACC is a council, not an open conference. Each Church in its domestic deliberations spends much of its time listening to itself. In the Council, small though it is, members listen to the voices of the world-wide Church, expressed by people who, like themselves, speak with authenticity out of Christian experience in a local situation.

The standard of speech-making may not always be high, indeed many speak in their second language; but by the time the Council comes to voting, it is consensus in the Anglican family, as there represented, that is emerging, and not the voice of any one Church, or any group, or outside organization. It is this, perhaps, as much as anything, that makes the Council worthy of attention.

29 July 1973, Dublin   JOHN HOWE

1 UNITY AND ECUMENICAL AFFAIRS

1 THE TRUE DYNAMIC OF UNITY

Fifty-three years ago the Lambeth Conference appealed to all Christian people to attempt a new approach to reunion: 'to adopt a new point of view: to look up to reality as it is in God. The unity which we seek exists. It is in God, who is the perfection of unity, the one Father, the one Lord, the one Spirit, who gives life to the one Body . . . The fellowship of the members of the one Body exists. It is the work of God, not of man. We have only to discover it and to set free its activities' (Encyclical Letter, Lambeth 1920).

This is a salutary reminder that uniting the Church is not merely a matter of making and implementing plans, which involve doctrinal definitions and a way of uniting our ministries. This would be a fruitless exercise, unless we are able to glorify God by our love for one another, demonstrated in mutual forgiveness, by bearing one another's burdens, and by sharing gifts of the Spirit.

But must another fifty-three years pass before obedience leads more of us, like faithful Abraham, to risk ourselves with God in the new relationships to which he is calling us? A robust theology and experience of the Holy Spirit enables the Church to trust him and to be like a grain of wheat which falls into the earth and dies, so that it does not remain alone but bears much fruit. In this, too, God is glorified.

St John's first letter makes it clear that fellowship is central to the gospel message. He says he proclaims the good news, 'so that you may have fellowship with us, and our fellowship is with the Father and with his Son, Jesus Christ', (1 John 1.3). The Holy Spirit leads us as sons to share in the love of the Father and the Son, and in turn to share this love with other men. Unity therefore is central to our Christian discipleship.

Thus in spite of all that may divide men, Christians are made into one Body in the love of God. The unity of this Body will be shown by a common faith, an ordained ministry recognized by all, joyful communion together, and a ministry in Christ's name to all the world. The presence with them of Jesus in whom 'all things were created in heaven and on earth' (Col. 1.16) will ensure a wide freedom to express a rich diversity in worship and service within his Body, the Church.

We are at this time compelled to recognize gladly the reality and vigour of Christian life beyond the boundaries of traditional Churches. From such experience of faith and life we have much to learn in the way of spontaneity, and a concern for the sharing of our faith. But we believe equally firmly that historical continuity and tradition remain essential qualities of the Church.

2 THE PRESENT SITUATION

Since the meeting at Limuru there has been some progress in church negotiations as well as some hindrances (see pp. 9–12). The present ecumenical scene presents both great cause for thankfulness and also a certain frustration. Churches and traditions are now involved with one another in a new way. Christians have been losing the old divisive self-consciousness and their awareness of being fellow-Christians has increased immeasurably. In the most recent years the breakthrough in relations between Roman Catholics and other Christians has happened in a way that would have been scarcely predictable only a decade ago. A few plans for united Churches have come to fruition, but others have run into delay and frustration; and this is why many are asking in some bewilderment: Where do we go from here?

A number of causes may lie behind this frustration. There is the scepticism of many young Christians about church structures in themselves, together with a lack of interest in whether they are divided or united. There is the tendency to emphasize what Christians can do together here and now in the service of humanity, in evangelism, and in practical fellowship. There is a concentration upon the local unity of members of different Churches in experimental ways. These are all certainly among the causes of half-heartedness in the pursuit of reunion schemes. But we cannot overlook the fact that there is also the inbred conservatism within the Churches which causes a fear of losing their treasures of past identity.

There is indeed a sense in which it is right for Christians not to dwell upon the Church as an end in itself, as they pursue together those ends for which the Church exists in the worship of God, in the service of humanity, and in the spreading of the gospel. Yet it is necessary that the goal of actual church union should emerge again as a powerful motive. The co-operation of Christians is now in a phase which cries out for intercommunion; but local intercommunion may lead to confusion and even sectarianism unless there are more than local approaches to the unifying of ministries and Churches. There must be no shrinking from the conviction that, to use the New Delhi phrase, 'all in each place' should be one in ordered fellowship as well as in faith and sacrament. While avoiding any quest for uniformity or for centralization, we reaffirm the conviction that organic union in the sense of united Churches is a goal for which intercommunion alone or federation alone is no substitute.

In the quest of union there are still the problems concerning the relations between the historic episcopate and other traditions of ministry. These problems are likely to be solved if they are seen to belong to the interim until there comes about a union in which, without anyone's repudiation of God's grace and goodness in the past, the historic episcopate finds itself as the organ of unity in a new way.

3 INTERCOMMUNION NOW

In this interim period, as we have called it, Christians of different traditions, who join together in common service or witness or study, discover a unity which is often as real and deep as it may be unexpected. They want to celebrate this unity in Holy Communion together, and if the rules of their Church discourage or forbid this, they are apt either quietly to ignore or openly to repudiate the rules. Or they may keep their rules uneasily, doubting whether they are disobeying the Spirit.

This situation is likely to become common, and it raises questions for many Anglicans. If an Anglican receives Holy Communion at the hands of a minister not episcopally ordained, is he thereby repudiating the necessity of episcopal ordination, and being disloyal to the constant tradition of his own Church? Clearly he is showing his belief that this other Church is a part of Christ's Body, and that Christ is working in and through it. If it were not so, the question of communicating with these other Christians would not arise; but are we going further, and by our action implying that differences of faith and order with that Church are matters of indifference? Intercommunion need not have such a logical consequence. The grace of communion depends on God himself. Christ has promised to be present when two or three are gathered in his name, and where his people seek him in faith he responds. In fact it is we who are always responding to his initiative. We find his presence in his people. We experience his coming in their celebration of his sacrament.

But this does not imply that the order of the Church is of no importance. Each part of Christ's divided Church has its own convictions about right order as well as its own expression of the faith. Anglicans believe that bishops have a role as sacramental agents of the unity of the Body, in time and in the Church they serve, locally and more widely. We therefore, in our own Church, insist that the minister of the Eucharist should demonstrate, by his episcopal ordination, the unity and continuity of the Body. Within our Church we hold this rule invariably, although not always for identical theological reasons. Other Christians do not have this conviction, and we respect their position while longing to share with them our own. A distinguished Roman Catholic theologian has suggested that 'at the present day, and for most of us, our theological divergence is the effect of our loss of full communion' (Bishop B. C. Butler in David L. Edwards, *The British Churches turn to the Future*, p. 78). Communion between separated

3

bodies might well lead towards convergence. Some are now convinced that the practice of intercommunion, responsibly enjoyed, with a desire on both sides to find and do the will of Christ, need not be only the end of our search for unity, as some of us have long held, but perhaps also a most potent encouragement to persevere in that way. Intercommunion certainly implies acceptance of each other in Christ, but not an unqualified acceptance of each other's distinctive traditions and approach. We hold to our own traditions. We believe that they are in accord with what Christ wills for his Church. It is in our search for unity that we shall rediscover a common tradition more fully expressive of his intention for the whole Church.

4   A WAY AHEAD

We believe that local initiative is essential for progress towards organic union. We believe that it is equally necessary and urgent that there should be a firm and solemn commitment of Churches to one another at the national or regional level to end schism and seek God's way of union. Only if dioceses and Provinces commit themselves in this way, together with the other Churches in their area, can the will of the whole Church to move towards organic union express itself. Moreover, without it, proper scope and confidence cannot be given to local initiative. If such a commitment is made, the Churches can agree on guidelines for local unity and assist its progress, so that instead of leading to confusion and frustration, it can make its indispensable contribution to a coherent plan of union in the future, and enable all our people to play their part in working towards a union that not only allows for proper diversity but also assures agreement in essentials.

Some Provinces and Churches are considering a commitment of this kind through a Covenant or Declaration of Intent. We encourage them to persevere with their intention, and we recommend that this approach be seriously considered by other Churches of our Communion. We see it as essentially a faithful response to the goodness of the living God, who has given us our unity with all Christians in Jesus Christ, and will build on our obedience to lead us step by step to the goal of the visible unity that he wills for his Church.

5   UNIFICATION OF MINISTRIES

In view of the importance of the unification of the ministry in all plans for union we draw particular attention to the North India/Pakistan plan of union. The distinctive element in this plan was the provision

4

that the unification of the ministry should be a corporate act within a Church already united. This represented a basic change from any act of 'mutual commissioning' carried out between Churches still separate, and as a preliminary to union.

The weakness in earlier proposals has been that they appear inevitably to obscure the fundamental truth that the gifts of grace are from God alone. They leave all who are involved exposed to the temptations of spiritual pride, and leave unexorcized the suspicion that particular Churches may seem to claim to possess, or to have authority over, particular gifts of grace which others may lack. It has been found to be extremely difficult with such proposals to avoid the impression of discriminatory judgements on others. This is a difficulty which may even be aggravated when mutual courtesy demands the kind of statement of recognition which appears to relativize one's own convictions. Finally, the effect is to suggest an 'adding together' of diverse gifts rather than a creative event in which a new and richer experience may emerge.

These difficulties are overcome when there has been sufficient mutual recognition between Churches of the reality of God's gracious gifts to them, which enables them to accept each other before God in an act of union, and thereafter to provide together for the unification of their ministries. In the North India/Pakistan unions this was done in a corporate act of worship. In this, with grateful acknowledgement of God's grace already manifested in the Churches and their ministries when they were separate, there was a prayer of humble commitment to God that he might continue to all this favour and grant to each minister 'whatever of the fulness of Christ's grace, commission and authority' he might need for his further ministry. This corporate act, carried through with the laying on of the same hands on all without discrimination, provides the channels which have traditionally been used for the bestowing of spiritual gifts by God. But it includes no negative judgement on the past and clearly expresses a common and continuing dependence on the grace of God.

While the North India/Pakistan plan specifically disclaims the suggestion that its method is the only one possible to provide for a unified ministry, it would appear to have provided a model whereby what has long proved to be an impasse has been overcome.

Resolution 1 Unification of Ministries

The Council notes that the Acts of Unification of the Ministries in the Churches of North India and Pakistan have made it possible already for most of the Anglican Churches to enter without reservation into full communion with the united Churches. It commends these acts as models to other Churches engaged in the preparation of schemes of union.

6 FULL COMMUNION

Limuru Resolution 1 invited 'the member Churches to consider the theology of full communion and its implications'. Reports have so far been received from only three of the Churches, and it is not therefore possible to give a comprehensive account of developing Anglican opinion. Events since 1971, particularly in the matter of relationships with the CSI, have however supported the suggestion made at Limuru that the term 'full communion' requires much more flexible application than has hitherto been the case. In the past it has been used with precise reference to interchangeability of ministers and communicants. But it is increasingly realized that to be in communion with another Church should involve much more spiritual sharing than that, and also that Churches can have a very real and also sacramental fellowship, while at the same time accepting certain limitations required by their own discipline.

7 BILATERAL CONVERSATIONS

(a) ANGLICAN–LUTHERAN CONVERSATIONS

The paragraphs on the Eucharist and the ministry in the Anglican–Lutheran Report were considered. They were examined with the question especially in mind as to whether what was being said to the Lutherans differed from what was being said to the Roman Catholics. For example, if this Report is thought to be deficient in its statement of the eucharistic sacrifice, does this mean that it is in conflict with the more ample formulation in the Anglican–Roman Catholic Agreed Statement? Recognizing differences in emphasis, it was not considered that contradictory things were being said.

It was also noted that paragraph 96 of the Report gives more positive encouragement to reciprocal intercommunion than is given by LCR 47 of 1968.

All the member Churches in considering this Report are asked to 'base their decisions not only on the human efforts which we have made but on their trust in the one living Lord of the Church' (*Anglican–Lutheran International Conversations*, Section 16).

The Conversations have been valuable in breaking the comparative isolation from each other of Anglicans and Lutherans. Local conversations have also commenced, as in South Australia.

Resolution 2   Anglican–Lutheran Conversations

This Council

(i) receives with satisfaction the Report of the Anglican–Lutheran International Conversations (1970/72) and commends it to the member Churches for consideration;

(ii) approves of the setting up of the Anglican–Lutheran Joint Working Group to receive and examine the comments from the Churches; and to take account of other inter-Church conversations in which Anglicans and Lutherans are involved;

(iii) recommends that it will be essential to allow proper time for the Churches to report their response to the Joint Working Group.

(b) ANGLICAN–OLD CATHOLIC CONVERSATIONS

The Council notes with satisfaction that conversations between Anglicans and Old Catholics are in progress, and that these cover practical co-operation in areas where members of our Churches live side by side.

Resolution 3   Exchange of Information between Commissions

The Council requests the Anglican–Roman Catholic and the Anglican–Orthodox International Commissions to keep those engaged in the Anglican–Old Catholic Conversations informed of their progress.

(c) THE COMMISSION FOR ANGLICAN–ORTHODOX JOINT DOCTRINAL DISCUSSIONS

The Council received the interim report of the Anglican–Orthodox Subcommission meeting at Chambésy in September 1972. The Council also received a communiqué on the first meeting of the full Commission held in July 1973. It is delighted that the Commission is now at work and to know that the next full meeting is planned for 1976. The Council is appreciative of the course the conversations are taking, and looks forward with keen anticipation to receiving further reports on its progress.

The Council hopes that in areas where there are both Anglican and Orthodox Churches increasingly close relationships will be encouraged.

Resolution 4   Anglican–Orthodox Conversations

The Council receives the interim report of the Anglican–Orthodox Joint Doctrinal Commission and commends the continuing dialogue to the prayer and study of the member Churches.

(d) ANGLICAN–ROMAN CATHOLIC CONVERSATIONS
  (i) *The ARCIC Statement on the Eucharist*

The Council received the Agreed Statement on Eucharistic Doctrine of the Anglican–Roman Catholic International Commission (ARCIC). The reactions of all the member Churches will be taken into account by ARCIC in any revised version of the Statement. Attention is drawn to the recent publication of the background documents to the Statement (e.g. in *One in Christ*, June 1973).

7

The Council wishes to record its satisfaction with the work of ARCIC; and looks forward to the prospect of an Agreed Statement on the Ministry in the near future.

Resolution 5   ARCIC Statement on the Eucharist

The Council welcomes the ARCIC Agreed Statement on Eucharistic Doctrine. It recommends the Statement to the consideration of all member Churches and asks those Churches which have not already reported their response to the Secretary General to do so.

(ii) *Anglican–Roman Catholic Commission on the Theology of Marriage* (*with its application to inter-Church marriages*)

The Council welcomes the work of the Anglican–Roman Catholic Commission on the Theology of Marriage. It looks forward to the completion of the Commission's task in view of its importance to the parties in an inter-Church marriage. The Council asks the Commission to note that conditions in Africa differ in many respects from those of the West in relation to inter-Church marriage discipline. It would seem, moreover, that there is considerable difference in the application of Roman Catholic marriage discipline in this matter from place to place.

The Council recommends that whenever possible local joint consultations on the subject of inter-Church marriages should be held, and encourages the Churches of the Anglican Communion to take the initiative. The Council has heard with grateful expectation of the proposed conference between Roman Catholic and other Churches in Ireland later this year.

Resolution 6   Commission on the Theology of Marriage

The Council resolves that on the Anglican side the work of the Anglican–Roman Catholic Commission on the Theology of Marriage shall continue under the aegis of the Council until its work is done.

(e) ARRANGEMENTS FOR BILATERAL CONVERSATIONS

By no. 5 of its Terms of Reference the Council is responsible for 'making arrangements for the conduct of pan–Anglican conversations'. The Council approved the following recommendation from the Standing Committee:

(i) Reports and statements from Commissions to be received by the President of the Council, the Archbishop of Canterbury, and the Secretary General to be responsible for their transmission to the Churches.

The Council, at its first subsequent meeting, would then consider the report in the light of information received from the member Churches.

(ii) The appointment of members to Commissions to be by the President and Secretary General in consultation with the Primates of the Anglican Communion.

8 MAR THOMA SYRIAN CHURCH

The Mar Thoma Church in South India has requested to enter into a relationship of full communion with the Churches of the Anglican Communion.

Resolution 7   Mar Thoma Church

The Council encourages Churches of the Anglican Communion to enter into the same kind of relationship with the Mar Thoma Syrian Church as that which most of them already enjoy with the Old Catholic and other Churches in terms of the Bonn Agreement.

9 UNION SCHEMES

(a) THE CANADIAN PLAN OF UNION

In response to the request of the Anglican Church of Canada for the Council's observations on the Plan of Union, careful consideration was given to the proposals and the following points made:

(i) While recognizing the complexities of the continuing debate in the Anglican Communion on Christian initiation, it is nevertheless considered that the double laying on of hands proposed in connection with infant baptism and confirmation is likely to lead to confusion.

It is thought desirable that the bishop should be directly or indirectly related to the rite of initiation.

(ii) Paragraph 57   In this and in other plans for reunion it would be preferable if a provision that the consecrated elements remaining after the communion of the people be reverently consumed rather than disposed of in some other way.

(iii) Paragraph 83   Although the proposal that a presbyter may seek admission to the order of deacon is a novel one, it is not thought that it will cause great difficulties in relationships with other Churches of the Anglican Communion.

(iv) Paragraph 146   One of the principal contributions of the Anglican Communion to the life of a united Church is the constitutional episcopate. It is noted that the Canadian Plan gives considerable attention to this matter. What follows is intended to underline this.

For Anglicans the bishop is not primarily an administrator. His role is more like that of a Father speaking for his own family, but acting always in and through the family's constitutional pattern. The bishop is regarded not only as a symbol but as an agent of the Church unity within and between dioceses. The bishop's sacramental function is the sign of this responsibility. The Council is anxious that the particular pastoral and teaching ministry of the bishop should be preserved. It would hope that this conception of the pastoral and sacramental and teaching functions of the bishops of the Church might be reflected and expressed throughout the structure of a united Church.

(v) *Appendix 1   The Services of Inauguration*
The Council would refer to what has been said above about the unification of ministries in Resolution 1 (p. 5).

(vi) *Appendix 2   The Ordinal*
If ordinals were constructed after a common pattern, it would make it easier for Churches to enter into relationships of full communion. This would be a valuable contribution to unity throughout the world. The ordinal of the Church of South India is commended as a model to be imitated.

Resolution 8   Canadian Plan of Union
The Council considered the Canadian Plan of Union and asks the Anglican Church of Canada to take note of the observations made in this Report.

(b)   GHANA CHURCH UNION
The Council notes with appreciation and satisfaction the alterations made by the negotiating Churches in the Ghana Church Union Scheme in its Service for the Unification of Ministries. The form of words now proposed is consistent with recommendations made by Lambeth 1958 and 1968.

It is also noted that the term 'Pastor' is used for the second order of the ministry. As the functions described are clearly those of a presbyter, it is considered that this use of the title 'Pastor' is acceptable.

The Council notes the proposal that persons other than ordained ministers may be authorized to celebrate the Holy Communion in certain circumstances. It believes that this will certainly create an obstacle to many Churches of the Anglican Communion entering into a relationship of full communion with a united Church in Ghana.

Resolution 9   Ghana Church Union
The Council encourages the dioceses in Ghana to continue in the negotiations and draws their attention to the difficulties that would be caused if lay celebration of Holy Communion were allowed in the united Church.

(c) REPORT ON UNITY NEGOTIATIONS

(i) In February 1973 the *Plan of Union and By-Laws* was published by the Anglican Church of *Canada*, the Christian Church (Disciples of Christ in Canada), and the United Church of Canada, for study of those Churches (see pp. 9-10 above).

(ii) In Sri Lanka (*Ceylon*) final assent to union had been given by all the negotiating Churches, but the inauguration of the united Church planned for Advent 1972 did not take place owing to a legal action against the diocese of Colombo which is expected to be heard in August 1973. In the meantime efforts are being made to increase co-operation between the Churches in mission and pastoral care so that the transition to the united Church will be more natural and effective.

(iii) In May 1972 the Anglican–Methodist Plan failed to achieve the required majority of votes in the General Synod of the Church of *England*, but it is hoped that the multi-Church approach by the new United Reformed Church (composed of former Presbyterians and Congregationalists) will have more success.

(iv) The *Ghana* Church Union Committee hopes to complete its proposals in July 1973 for study by the negotiating Churches (see p. 10 above).

(v) In 1973 the Negotiating Committees of the Church of *Ireland*, the Presbyterian Church in Ireland, and the Methodist Church in Ireland, after five years of tripartite conversations, issued an Agreed Statement entitled *Towards a United Church*.

(vi) In *Kenya* and *Tanzania* despite the breakdown of talks between Anglicans, Lutherans, Presbyterians, Methodists, and Moravians, a certain amount of understanding and education has been achieved, and the Archbishop of Kenya is planning to ask for a resumption of talks.

(vii) In *New Zealand* a referendum late in 1972 gave a 58% vote for the Plan of Union, and the diocesan synods are in process of voting upon it. Final decisions will be made by the General Synod in 1974.

(viii) Since the ending of the civil war in *Nigeria* church union negotiations have been resumed and two meetings have been held.

(ix) In *Scotland* conversations between the Church of Scotland and the Episcopal Church continue. Six Churches, including the Scottish Episcopal Church, have been engaged in multilateral conversations. An interim report entitled *Multilateral Church Conversation in Scotland* has been produced for consideration by the member Churches. A Study Group consisting of members of the Episcopal Church and the Roman Catholic Church has been formed, which is expected to report in the autumn of 1973.

(x)   In August 1972 *A Plan of Union* was published in *South Africa*. Six Churches are involved in this and the Anglican Provincial Synod will take a vote in November 1973.

(xi) In the *USA* a study of and response to the Consultation's *Plan of Union* has been its major programme for the past three years. Deeper study will continue, but initial findings have shaped the Consultation's immediate future, which includes two proposals relating to 'Generating Communities' and 'Interim Eucharistic Fellowship'. These proposals suggest means by which representatives of the participating Churches through local initiative may have the experience of common life, service, and worship. The United Presbyterian Church, which withdrew from the Consultation in 1972, has since rejoined it.

(xii) The Joint Committee of the Churches in *Wales* has produced *Covenanting for Union in Wales*. Final decision is expected in 1974.

10   ANGLICAN CENTRE IN ROME

Resolution 10   Anglican Centre in Rome

The Council warmly appreciates the past and present work of the Anglican Centre in Rome and its successive Directors. It hopes that this work will continue vigorously and that the Council of the Centre will consider how it may be promoted and extended. It emphasizes the importance of discussion with the Secretariat for Promoting Christian Unity in Rome, and the development of consultation with other departments of the Curia. It urges that proper financial provision be made for the activities of the Centre and its Director.

11   LIAISON WITH THE WORLD COUNCIL OF CHURCHES

The system of communication between the Secretary General's office and the WCC Secretariat in Geneva has proved very worthwhile, and is valued by both sides. From the retirement of Mr Robert Beloe in 1971, Miss Janet Lacey acted as liaison officer. These duties have now been taken over by the Reverend David Chaplin. The Council wishes to record its grateful appreciation of Miss Janet Lacey as its liaison officer with the WCC.

12   ALLOCATION OF ANGLICAN PLACES ON THE ASSEMBLY OF THE WCC

Consequent upon Limuru Resolution 12 the Council considered and approved a draft allocation within the Communion of the fifty-nine places on the WCC Assembly assigned to the Anglican Communion.

This allocation will be submitted for final approval to the Central Committee of the WCC.

Resolution 11   Unity and Ecumenical Affairs
The Council commends the report on Unity and Ecumenical Affairs for study by all the member Churches, drawing particular attention to what is said about:

(*a*) The true dynamic of unity
(*b*) The present situation
(*c*) Intercommunion now
(*d*) A way ahead
(*e*) The unification of ministries.

2 CHURCH AND SOCIETY

Part A: Education:
A Process of Liberation for Social Justice

A PERSONAL NOTE FROM THE SECTION
We have engaged in a process of learning and grown in fellowship in so doing. We have considered the concrete situations in which we are involved; the struggles and aspirations of our fellow men who are seeking to attain to liberation which is national, international, and fully human. We have perceived more clearly our personal attitudes in the face of the pressures and the alternative options we face. We have grappled with each other to discern the further implications which challenge us to deeper commitment in our respective situations; and to evolve a common vision of the goals towards which we must strive if we are to mature in our Christian discipleship in the days ahead.

In all this we share much in common with our fellow men who face similar situations. But we also have distinctive Christian perspectives centred on the words and works of Jesus Christ, and unique sacramental fellowship centred on his continuing Presence in our midst.

1 VIOLENCE IN THE HUMAN SITUATION

It is necessary to understand that the injustice that exists in pluralist societies is violent by nature. It violates the freedom of man *to be* and this includes both the oppressor and the oppressed. This is not a new finding, for Limuru in Section 3 of its Church and Society report, and the Uppsala Assembly of the World Council of Churches have made this same point. However it is a fact which we consistently avoid facing.

One example is our violent, selfish, and short-term use of natural resources and the consequent problem of pollution. Violent injustice also exists where the imposition upon people of political, social, economic, cultural, or religious structures dehumanizes both groups, the oppressed and the oppressors. Powerlessness on the part of some and their inability to express their pain violates their freedom to pursue their own proper ends. It leaves them open to destructive exploitation.

The problems of human communication contribute to such injustice. In many instances the distortion or simple lack of information between different social groups results in a cruel and inhuman exploitation of the one by the other. But cases of human injustice are not simply issues of communication. They are in fact ultimately expressions of the social nature of sin.

Christians and the Church must care more for the well-being of persons and human community than for their own safety; they must

14

care for non-Christians as well as for Christians. In many parts of the 'Third World' the vision has arisen of the liberation of people from all that enslaves or degrades them in their personal and social lives. This vision is moulded by differing cultural emphases and traditions. But in all of them there is the notion that social liberation to achieve development and justice must be linked with personal liberation from all that enslaves the heart of man. Christians who share this vision think in terms of the biblical images of the Kingdom of God, of a new heaven and a new earth.

All committed Christians seeking the coming of the Kingdom in their particular situations are faced with serious moral choices which involve painful decisions. The role of Christians and church leaders is to encourage committed Christian groups holding diverse opinions to maintain a diaglogue within the one Christian fellowship in spite of the tensions between them. We deplore attempts at maintaining an unreal neutrality. We urge Christians and church leaders to make courageous commitments in favour of social justice in their particular situations.

In all this our quest must be for total human development by the grace of God. The way of the Christian is to press towards that 'mature manhood measured by nothing less than the full stature of Christ' (Eph. 4.13). We are aware of lopsided emphases within the Church in the work of spiritual formation, resulting often in faith being used as a buffer against life's problems. We believe that spiritual formation based on the redeeming work of Jesus Christ opens Christians to God's transforming goodness. This happens in the midst of the frustrations and hopes of life in society now.

2   NATIONAL DEVELOPMENT IN THE INTERNATIONAL SITUATION

The development of any nation is a two-way process. It aims at self-reliance and at the involvement of the people in the search for techniques which will utilize responsibly indigenous human and material resources. We urge Christians to be aware of the sacrifices and austerities which may result from embargoes on imports or the imposition of higher taxes as part of the price of promoting national development.

The current systems of trade and aid controlled by the developed countries work to their advantage. Restrictive conditions are laid down when loans are made by international monetary agencies to developing countries. Rich countries should seek to bring about changes in the pattern of international trade so that this unfair benefit can be removed. We regret that many of the rich nations have not as yet achieved a minimal target of 1 % of their Gross National Product to be used in assisting poorer nations to reach a goal of balanced agricultural and industrial growth and an equitable distribution of income.

15

Christians and Churches of the rich nations must take seriously their responsibility to persuade their respective governments to bring about reforms in these situations as soon as possible. They must awaken their fellow-citizens to accept the sacrifices involved.

Development in the rich nations has been based on the model of maximizing national economic growth. The human cost of such rampant economic growth is too high. It results in grave damage through the squandering of natural resources, the indiscriminate growth of a consumer mentality, and the ruthless disposal of polluting effluents. Churches must awaken their members to this perilous course of events and seek to initiate effective action.

Agencies involved in assisting development projects should be encouraged by the Churches to give financial support to oppressed groups which are working for a more just and equitable society. Churches engaged in development projects should not unthinkingly co-operate with government-initiated projects for development. They should refuse to participate in development projects which do not serve the purposes of social justice.

Christian and secular agencies and affluent local churches should accept austerities in their administrative budgets and in the life style of their officers to demonstrate their solidarity with the development of the poorer nations. These economies will enhance the value of the work done and benefit the integrity of the worker.

There are various models of national development. With initiative from élitist groups who control power the State may itself bring about the transference of resources. Oppressed groups within nations may work for the transference of power and resources. Sometimes this transference may be accompanied by violence. On other occasions it may involve a non-violent method of mutual sharing.

Resolution 12   Social Justice

The Council calls upon its member Churches:

(a) to be sensitive to the violent dehumanization of minority peoples in their midst;

(b) to acknowledge the Church's vocation to side with the oppressed in empowering them to live their own lives in freedom, even at some sacrifice to itself, while at the same time seeking in the power of Christian love to bring about the true liberation of the oppressor;

(c) to seek for the education of the majority in these needs by confrontation with and participation in the suffering of the oppressed;

(d) that where solutions to such violence seem possible (as, for example, in the pollution of our environment by industry or testing of nuclear devices), to join with those pressing for such resolution;

(e) where apparent resolutions are not available, to serve as an agency for demanding that attention is not averted, through either fear or fatigue, from the persistent and hopeful quest of a just settlement.

3 A THEOLOGY OF LIBERATION IN THE CONTEMPORARY SITUATION

(a) Theological Reflection—
a Response to the Person and Work of Jesus Christ

This theological reflection relates to the attitudes and proposals we were led to adopt in dealing with our particular situations and the topics assigned. It is not meant to reflect a total interpretation of the gospel of Jesus Christ. Nor is it meant to be descriptive of the variety of interpretations of the biblical texts quoted. It is a response to the Person and work of the unique Jesus Christ from the perspective of the insights and challenges emerging in the contemporary situation. There is an undoubted interaction between this reflection, the situations we have analysed, and the proposals we have developed.

We based our reflection on the words and actions of Jesus Christ as they have come to us, and discovered that some of us do not find the life-situation of the historical Jesus very alien from our own. We are aware that others find his life-situation more alien from their own and are hesitant to make use of his words and actions in their theological reflections. We would nevertheless encourage them to do so.

Jesus emerges in the pages of the Gospel as the expected and inspired Saviour of men. According to the prophetic tradition this implies the liberation of his people and the bringing about of justice, as well as a liberation from death, sin, law, and demonic powers. He shared their religious and cultural heritage, their present struggles and their future expectations (Luke 4.14–19; cf. Isa. 61.1). The themes stated in his recorded 'policy statement' in Nazareth cover the whole of personal and social life, and envisage the inauguration of the era of salvation. They can be correlated with the vision of Mary in the Magnificat (Luke 1.46ff), who praises the Lord for the radical changes in economic, political, and social structures; with the vision of Zachariah, who rejoices at the freedom of his people and the well-being which flows from the forgiveness of sins and the knowledge and service of God (Luke 1.68–79); with the expectation of the Psalmists and Prophets who yearn for the era of social justice, development of natural resources, and well-being in community (cf. Pss. 144.12–15; 146.5–10; Isa. 35.5–7; 58.6–7).

Jesus had such an openness to the mind and will of his Father, and a similar love-centred openness to the varied needs of his fellow men, that he experienced the human predicament in all its depth. He was therefore able to share in the expectations of his fellow men, and also

17

to redefine these expectations from his own unique perspective in a way that has a continuing relevance for all men in all societies.

Jesus preached the good news of release not only to the poor. He also communicated it to the rascally rich such as Zacchaeus who was released from the guilt and power of sin. He supported the exploited and alienated in his denunciations when he cleansed the Temple with a whip. But when they brought him the tribute money, he gave a reply that did not give clear support to the revolutionary nationalist party of the Zealots. He showed by word and deed that we must love our enemies who despise or oppress us; that we must love to the end in the midst of bitterness and betrayal. He not only announced the era of liberation initiated by God, but also inaugurated it by laying down his life through humiliation, crucifixion, and death in obedience to his Father's will.

St Paul, reflecting on all this after Christ's triumphant risen Presence was made known, described him as the new man (new Adam). Jesus had reached perfect manhood through the struggles and sufferings he underwent to enable others to be changed into new men and women (Heb. 2.10–end). Jesus was the source, guide, and goal of salvation from all forms of sin, and he brings to birth the new man in the new social and natural order (Rom. 8.18–25), which he described as 'the Kingdom'. He opens the way for others to enter into union with his Father, so that they are empowered to transform his world under the leading of his Spirit and to grow into his likeness. The last chapters of the Book of Revelation contain passages reminding us that this transformation of man, society, and nature can come to perfection only through God's own action.

(b) Theological Guidelines

Jesus Christ calls all men to share in the fullness of life with God and their fellow men. 'I have come that they may have life, and may have it in all its fullness' (John 10.10).

He also teaches us to reach fullness of life by learning to perceive and use our hidden resources through involvement, honest confrontation, reflection, and action in our particular situations, for example, Jesus dealing with the woman of Samaria (John 4.4–30); God dealing with Peter in Caesarea (Acts 10.9–23). This has both personal and social implications and an eschatalogical aspect in that it is God's achievement in the end. Human obedience now, in and through Jesus Christ, can result in the first fruits of the new creation.

The conversion and reconciliation of conflicting individuals and groups within society, freeing them to discover the fullness of human life which Christ offers them, is an urgent task (Eph. 4.13; Col. 1.28). In part this consists in the freeing of man from all domination, dependence, and discrimination which deprive him of the vocation to which

God has called him. We believe that this goal can be realized only when we are involved in actual experiences of such conflict. These educate us to a deeper sensitivity to the feelings of our opponents and to new life styles that will engender reconciliation.

Our life in the Church dramatizes our belief that mankind is as one human body under God. If one member is hurt, the whole body suffers (1 Cor. 12.12–27). Therefore no one lacks responsibility for the pain of his brother; it is the vocation of the Christian to be alongside the oppressed (Matt. 25.31–46). This responsibility extends to man's common life with the whole of creation (Rom. 8.18–21; Isa. 11.6–9).

In responding to the suffering of the oppressed it is important that Christians recognize not only the concept of reconciliation, but also a concept of 'chaos'. If a just order is our goal, it is necessary that Christians struggle on through conflict, tension, suffering, and chaos towards the final hope of reconciliation. As inheritors of the Kingdom, which takes the form of a new heaven and a new earth, our hope is a confident expectation in 'God's ordering Word'. Our hope sustains us in the sacrificial ministry of reconciliation which embodies the final victory over social injustice and personal death (Jon. 2.1–9; Rom. 8.18; Eph. 4.8–10; 2 Pet. 3.5–7; Gen. 1.2–3).

As a specific and timely illustration, we are thankful for all the efforts being made to achieve reconciliation in Northern Ireland by sensitive Christian people and leaders. We hope that the effect of these efforts in Church and State will be the achievement of peace with justice for the North Irish people.

(c) Word and Sacrament as Effective Signs

Jesus gives us an example to follow, a vision to see, and a goal to reach. His abiding Spirit inspires, cleanses, and renews us in the midst of our failures, to press on with our eyes fixed on him who is the 'source, guide and goal of all that is' (Rom. 11.36). In the Scriptures he gives us a means of clearing and renewing our vision. In the two gospel sacraments of Baptism and Eucharist he provides a means of dying with him to all that is evil in our persons and social structures, and of rising to newness of personal and corporate life. They are means of celebrating our offering of life and work to him in our on-going discipleship. The dramatic action of these sacramental rites can be used much more imaginatively and effectively to express the successive stages of our continuing Christian life. When accompanied by vibrant song, art, and dance, they can be made to express our underlying joy in following Jesus amidst our anxieties and failures.

In this spirit we call our fellow-Anglicans to commit themselves with us to following Jesus in the work of liberation for personal and social renewal, justice, development, and wholeness of life in our respective societies.

Resolution 13   Christian Structures and Life-Style

Church institutions and leaders should critically examine their extravagant structures and life style in the light of Jesus' example, to demonstrate their solidarity with their fellows who suffer oppression and poverty.

Resolution 14   New Methods of Bible Study and Liturgy

The changing pattern of society demands that the Churches seek and engage in new methods of Bible study and liturgy to uncover their power for our times as revelatory instruments of the unique Christ.

4   EDUCATION IN HUMAN DEVELOPMENT

All over the world today education has become a major instrument for the development of individuals and communities. Many nations, especially the developing countries, spend large portions of their national income on education. The Church, both by nature and tradition, is one of the most powerful educational agencies, equipped especially in the developed parts of the world with massive material resources. This puts a heavy responsibility on the Church to reappraise its role in education at a time when inherited approaches and systems in education are undergoing a serious crisis and have come under severe criticism.

The deepest crisis facing education today is the lack of clarity regarding the goals of education. While sharing in this uncertainty, the Church needs to make a serious effort to help answer the question: What is education for?

(a) A Challenge to Assumptions about Education

The Church is challenged *to review its own assumptions with regard to its roles* vis-à-vis *public education and with regard to its own educational programmes.* A clear response to this challenge is especially vital in situations where people suffer from political and economic oppression, influenced by racist and religious discrimination; and where education is often used as a tool for oppression and indoctrination.

Education is no end in itself and therefore it is never a neutral process. Education basically is used either to *domesticate* or to *liberate* man. It is always carried out within the context of the struggle of a community or a nation to achieve its own goals. To be authentic, these goals should be formulated and reformulated through processes of political participation in which everyone is able to share. Involvement in such decision-making processes is a primary prerequisite for a relevant education. Education is relevant in as far as it enables people to 'become aware of their own problems, weigh the possibilities that are open to them, and choose their own course of action with regard to their duty to society' (WCC, Bangkok Assembly, 1973). Linking education to social and political involvement means it must be a life-long learning-process.

The Church has often failed to recognize the intrinsic link between education, political self-determination, and social responsibility. We have often been, and often still are, on the side of those who determine value-systems and educational goals *for* others instead of *with* others. In many situations our Churches are allied with the minority élite in power, determining what the majority of people should be educated for. However, if we are to serve people educationally rather than impose, and to liberate them instead of domesticating them, we must establish a partnership with those seeking knowledge in a process to determine the goals and methods of education. This implies a critical view of our relationship to the power-élites in our societies, and a reappraisal of our educational goals and methods, and of the processes by which they are defined.

With sorrow we acknowledge that too often the Church is involved in education which is mainly oriented towards the promotion of the society within which it works, without sufficient concern for the political aspirations, economic needs, and cultural heritages of other peoples, especially the poor and oppressed. The growing political, economic, and cultural interdependence in our emerging world-community must receive due attention in a relevant education for development, both in developed and developing countries. Education must evolve a critical consciousness with regard to the value-systems behind various concepts of development which are propagated by governments both in developing and developed countries. The Churches must never blindly follow such propaganda, but highlight the concern that the development of the whole person, and the growth of sensitivity and responsibility towards the underprivileged, must be the centre of any education for human development. This implies a critical re-appraisal of the Churches' involvement in a formal élitist education, which emphasizes personal advancement and lacks sympathy with the underschooled and unskilled. Education must be geared towards education for the masses, and emphasize their need for the develop-ment of practical skills in order to earn their living.

(b) Education for Liberation

In many areas of the world political and economic systems exercise oppression in denying minorities or even the majority of people the right to shape their future. Such situations are often characterized by structural oppression. In South Africa the vast majority of the Black population is deprived systematically of its basic rights by political oppression, economic exploitation, and educational deprivation based on structures of racist discrimination. In other parts of Africa, in Asia, Europe, North and Latin America, minorities are being oppressed and deprived of basic human rights because of religious or ethnic discrimination. In many situations of oppression and discrimination the educational system becomes a primary tool of indoctrination in order to perpetuate the existing power-structure. Schooling then serves mainly to increase the domesticating character of the oppressive system by teaching people *what* to think instead of *how* to think. For example, in South Africa the basic educational needs of the Black people are ignored or refused, the conditions of educational facilities are extremely poor, and school fees for Black people make it virtually impossible for most of them to receive education. In societies where minorities are oppressed for racial, religious, or ethnic reasons, their feelings, values, and needs are deliberately neglected.

In such situations people seeking truth which liberates must heavily rely on non-formal education. They can achieve that goal only if they learn to help themselves. Programmes of community-organization, awareness-building ('conscientization') in connection with cultural and social analysis, adult education programmes and leadership development, complement or substitute for a school education which is insensitive and hostile towards the needs of the oppressed. Especially in these situations the Churches must seek ways to develop or support non-formal educational programmes. It may mean in some situations a discontinuation of school-based education by the Churches, and a focus on alternatives to traditional schooling.

Education for liberation will not be fulfilled until the oppressor is confronted with the full meaning of his violence on the person of the oppressed. This confrontation will necessarily require the creative conflict and sacrifice which is characteristic of the risk of the cross (Matt. 16.24–6). We recognize that this is an action which goes against the grain for all except those who are willing to trust God, and that in some situations the time for confrontation is not yet fulfilled.

Where few apparent social, political, or economic solutions to the problems of violence exist, the demand for the dominant group to be sensitive to and responsible about the freedom of the oppressed remains. Education of the oppressor is often only possible as we participate with the oppressed in the violence done to him (Luke 4.16–19). It follows that the Church must be willing to confront its own ecclesiastical structures with their oppressive role, and learn again the role of the servant (e.g. the place of youth in the Church).

The oppressed ultimately have to take the lead in the dialogue with the oppressors; and the role of the Church is to facilitate the dialogue. At times this means bringing the oppressed and the oppressors face to face with one another. By entering into dialogue, the oppressor can begin the process of giving up the privileges of dominance.

Where solutions do not appear, it may be necessary to accept our powerlessness, to recognize the anger associated with it, and to struggle together through it (2 Cor. 12.9). For our conviction is that only among those who are restless for the Kingdom will God's word be heard and obeyed. We must not seek simple halfway solutions or deceptive palliatives.

Resolution 15   Programmes of Education

(*a*) The Churches of the Anglican Communion should educate their members to accept the sacrifices involved in the initiation of political, social, and economic reforms, and show an openness of attitude towards oppressed groups in their struggle for social justice.

(*b*) The Churches should give high priority to the development of educational programmes for liberation and social justice. In particular, we recommend that the Churches:

(i) review critically their involvement in public (general) educational systems, and in particular in church schools;

(ii) in all continents give high priority in the field of education to non-formal educational programmes, and initiate new forms of education for liberation, making use of the recently developed approaches and concepts worked out especially in Asia, Africa, and Latin America—e.g. 'village as school' approach, community-organization, awareness-building ('conscientization'), lay-training centres;

(iii) make use of all available facilities in the field of educational experimentation and research, including the use of WCC, UNESCO, and other conference material;

(iv) promote the production of educational materials in print, audio-visual aids, role-play methods, and other media, in order to foster information and communication among their membership as well as the wider public.

(*c*) The Churches should set about a fresh approach to such programmes of education for social justice by:

(i) identifying areas of oppression;

(ii) offering their facilities for dialogue between oppressors and oppressed, and using their contacts and influence to bring this about;

(iii) training those who will act as mediators to sustain these dialogues at a deep level;

(iv) finding forms of organizing creative confrontation where dialogue is not possible.

23

Resolution 16   Employment Schemes

As a means of seeking to achieve a liberated and just society, the Churches should become actively involved in schemes which provide employment opportunities for unemployed people, particularly the school and university leavers.

Resolution 17   Allocation of Gross National Product

The Council calls upon member Churches in developed countries, which have not yet achieved a minimal target of the allocation of 1 % of Gross National Product for the assistance of poorer nations achieving balanced growth, to do all in their power to educate and assist their adherents to bring pressure upon governments to achieve such a target.

Resolution 18   Investment Policy

As an example of the responsible use of power, the Council urges the member Churches, particularly in the more affluent countries, to examine their investment portfolios and bank deposits for the purpose of influencing, through the exercise of stock resolutions and other comparable means (not excluding divestment), the management practices of companies and multi-national corporations in which church funds are invested or deposited, to the end that heightened sensitivity to social goals, including environmental concerns, be furthered, and social justice be served; and where possible to integrate such practices with those of other church bodies.

Part B   A Reply to a Memorandum from the Episcopal Synod of the Church of the Province of South Africa

(See Appendix 2, pp. 26-9 below)

The Anglican Consultative Council at Dublin resolves to continue to seek ways of implementing the 1968 Lambeth Conference Resolution 16 which states:

Racism is a blatant denial of the Christian faith. (1) It denies the effectiveness of the reconciling work of Jesus Christ, through whose love all human diversities lose their divisive significance; (2) It denies our common humanity in creation and our belief that all men are made in God's image; (3) It falsely asserts that we find our significance in terms of racial identity rather than in Jesus Christ.

We affirm the Limuru decision to support the WCC Programme to Combat Racism (see pp. 25-6 below). We note the information from the bishops of the Province that there have been changes in the situation in two years when they say, 'Black leadership has now been given a constitutional role in the Reserves or Bantustans in South Africa', and 'successful strikes are evidence of the effective use of economic power by Africans who now find some support for their demands from leaders in their Bantustan Governments'. However, we are also aware that there are other Black leaders who have been banned or placed under house arrest and also are aware of the sinister circumstances concerning the trial of the former Dean of Johannesburg and of the banishment of Bishop Winter from South West Africa.

We would urge that the Programme be further extended to include a concern for poor and powerless groups, including minorities in parts of the world other than South Africa. Furthermore, additional grants should be made available through the Programme to Combat Racism, as well as other agencies, to help the families of political and war prisoners in numerous countries. Minority and oppressed groups in many parts of the world are engaged in a struggle for their legitimate social, legal, economic, and cultural rights, and many families of political and war prisoners are suffering.

While the initial Programme was intended to express a primary concern for white racism, we should remember racism includes conflict between black and white, white and black, brown and yellow, black and black.

We all share a solidarity of guilt, but as Christians we share Christ's redemption and also responsibility for his redemptive task in the world.

We would finally note with thankfulness the dialogue about to take place between representatives of the WCC and the South African Council of Churches, and would urge that such dialogue and consultation be entered into wherever possible with the National Councils of Churches prior to the adoption of any programme.

> *Carried. In favour 41, against 2, abstentions 4.*
>
> *Bishop B. B. Burnett and Bishop J. P. Burrough recorded dissenting votes.*

APPENDIX 1

The Resolution on Racism, referred to above, which was passed by the Council at Limuru in 1971 (Resolution No. 17, p. 28 of that Report) was as follows:

The Council resolves:

1. that individuals, Churches, and other institutions be encouraged to re-examine, in penitence, their lives and structures with a view to eradicating all forms of discrimination;

2. that the Churches of the Anglican Communion urgently seek ways of implementing Lambeth Conference Report, Resolution 16, and the World Council of Churches' programme to combat racism, on the understanding that the grants made thereunder will not be used for military purposes;

3. to send our warm greetings to the Churches engaged in the common struggle to combat racism and segregation in southern Africa and the United States of America, assuring them of our continuing prayers and encouragement;

4. to ask the member Churches to urge their governments to stop selling arms to all regimes which may use them to further racist policies, since such sales are repugnant to the Christian conscience and in defiance of the resolutions of the United Nations Security Council adopted in 1963 and reaffirmed in July 1970;

5. to ask member Churches to urge their governments to rescind all laws and regulations, whether in regard to immigration or continued residence in the country, which in practice discriminate against people on grounds of race or colour.

APPENDIX 2

A Memorandum for the Anglican Consultative Council from the Church of the Province of South Africa (March 1973)
World Council of Churches and Liberation Movements

The Church of the Province of South Africa readily endorses and supports effective programmes to combat racism. Together with other Churches in South Africa, the CPSA had purposefully taken the initiative and begun to move in this matter before the Programme to combat Racism was approved by the WCC. For example, *The Message to the People of South Africa*, which was prepared before Uppsala and published by the South African Council of Churches in September 1968, laid a theological foundation for the Church's witness as far as racism is concerned. The Study Project on Christianity in Apartheid Society was established in the following year to work out the practical implications of the theology of the *Message* in our life in Church and Society. The Human Relations and Reconciliation programme of the CPSA which was given its mandate by the Provincial Synod of November 1970 has now made a considerable impression on the life of the Church.

The CPSA believes, however, that the inclusion in the Programme to combat Racism of support for the non-military needs of liberation movements operating against Governments in Southern Africa was intended to demonstrate the WCC's identification with the aims of the guerillas. This would seem to be borne out by Mr Baldwin Sjollema's saying that the WCC's decision represented a decision by the Council 'to take the liberation movements seriously'. (*S. African Outlook*, Nov. 1970.) Had the WCC not desired to express its solidarity quite explicitly with the liberation movements the non-military needs of guerillas could have been met by the Department of

Inter-Church Aid. This indeed was the situation prior to the establishment of the Special Fund to combat Racism. It is not without significance that while the WCC operated in this way the member Churches in South Africa raised no objection.

It is abundantly clear, moreover, that the WCC's Special Fund is understood by both black and white people in Southern Africa as an identification of the Council with not only the aims of the liberation movement but also the means employed to achieve those aims. It is seen as a decision that the Church's traditional approach of working for justice and reconciliation has failed and that a new kind of power must be employed to find a 'solution'. Because, moreover, this is what the WCC intended and what grants to liberation movements are generally understood to mean, the official WCC representation of the Special Fund as being simply for humanitarian purposes is unsatisfactory and some would say even dishonest.

In view of the fact that the WCC clearly intended the Special Fund to demonstrate its support for liberation movements which are dedicated to violent change in Southern Africa, it is astonishing that the fund was inaugurated prior to the serious study of the use of violence by Christians for which the WCC has now made provision. It would seem that the decision to identify the WCC with liberation movements was taken on very dubious grounds.

Significant changes have begun to take place in South Africa in recent years. The ideology of apartheid has, ironically enough, established increasingly substantial platforms for the expression of Black opinion which are enabling Black power to become a factor in the formulation of policy in South Africa. The apartheid policy has in a variety of ways of set purpose and inadvertently developed Black consciousness. On the one hand Black consciousness has developed in reaction to apartheid and white power and on the other it has also been encouraged by the separate institutions required by apartheid.

The Church of the Province has also through its Human Relations and Reconciliation programme encouraged Black consciousness in order to enable its Black members to play a more effective role in the life of both Church and society. There has already been a significant change in attitudes and an increase in Black participation in policy-making bodies in many dioceses. As the programme penetrates more deeply into the life of dioceses and parishes more dramatic shifts in the Church's power structure will be experienced.

There is no doubt, moreover, that the growth of Black consciousness in the USA and the existence of Independent African States elsewhere in Africa have encouraged a more robust Black response to issues in Southern Africa than heretofore. This must be seen as solid gain and can only increase more effective Black participation in the use of power in South Africa. A more just society will emerge therefore as the fruit of an increasing application of pressure by South African Black people themselves.

Black leadership has now been given a constitutional role in the Reserves or Bantustans in South Africa. This means that Black people are now able to use constitutional channels for giving expression to their desire for change. This is inadequate machinery for bringing about immediate and dramatic changes, but it does give Blacks an opportunity to struggle to liberate themselves.

This is not the only avenue open for Africans to exert pressure for a more just society in South Africa. There have been several strikes by Black workers during 1972/73 which have resulted in improved wages and conditions of labour. These successful strikes are evidence of the effective use of economic power by Africans who now find some support for their demands from leaders in their Bantustan Governments.

In spite of the possibility of replacing workers by methods of automation there remains a very considerable power lever in the hands of Black workers simply because our lively economy is almost wholly dependent on Black labour. The exercise of this power is capable of producing significant changes in the balance of economic and ultimately also of political power in our Society. There are thus increasingly non-violent means of exercising power within South Africa which in time may well produce adjustments to the power structure in South Africa. The employment of these means, with courage and determination, are certain to produce wholesome change.

There are no short cuts to be found to secure the improvements in the quality of life which many desire. Furthermore the shifts and adjustments in policies and power which seem modest and undramatic may in the long run have far more radical consequences than perceived at the time.

The decision to give financial support to liberation movements in order to identify the WCC member Churches with them in spite of the opposition of Southern African member Churches is a violation of the spirit and it may be also of the letter of the Constitution and Rules of the WCC. One of the functions of the WCC is described as 'to support the Churches in their world-wide missionary and evangelistic task' (Section III, v). In Southern Africa, however, the Council is acting in defiance of the wishes of almost all the member Churches in that area and not in support of them. This kind of action would seem, moreover, to contradict the fourth paragraph of Section IV of the Constitution which says: 'The WCC shall not legislate for the Churches: nor shall it act for them in any manner except as indicated above or as may hereafter be specified by the constituent Churches.' The WCC is acting for the constituent Churches in Southern Africa in a manner not specified by them and without prior consultation with them.

If the policy and witness of its member Churches in South Africa are quite evidently opposed by the decision-making bodies of the WCC in a matter that specifically applies to them, it would seem that the consistent and honourable thing to do would be either to respect the integrity and obedience to God of member Churches or to exclude them from the Council's fellowship. The present policy of the WCC fails to respect the integrity of member Churches in Southern Africa and is destructive of fellowship with them.

It is very obvious that a great many Africans both in South Africa and elsewhere applaud the Programme to combat Racism. Many indeed have pleaded for support for the programme because, they say, unless the Church shows that it supports the aspirations of the liberation movements African Christians will drift away from the Churches. This may be true, but from a Christian point of view it bears no more weight than the fact that a majority of white people in South Africa deplore the decision of the WCC. It simply means that the WCC supports one nationalism against another and leaves one with the impression that the WCC decision is a response to political pressure rather than to what the gospel requires.

If there is truth in this judgment, and we believe there is more than is usually recognized, it means that the WCC may be more firmly gripped by the principalities and powers than it thinks; and it may be, quite as much as those who defend white power in Southern Africa. It is essential that not only South African Christians but the WCC gives its first and final loyalty to the Lord Jesus Christ.

The pressures of history can too easily be identified with the will of God. The result is that the Christian brotherhood is threatened with a breakdown in fellowship because Christians are not prepared to stand by one another in Christ irrespective of pressures exerted by 'the world'.

Such pressures can and do simply identify the salvation which is God's gift to us through Jesus Christ with particular social changes, developments, or resolutions and suggest that these programmes alone express the mission of Christ in our time. This rests on a false understanding of Christ's work and of the Kingdom of God. The Programme to combat Racism must face, as every other application of the gospel must, whether or not it is being true to the gospel at this point.

Faithfulness to the gospel of Jesus Christ lays upon black and white Christians alike the obligation to go outside the camps which loyalty to contending ideologies have erected in order to find one another and hold on to one another in the painful knowledge that loving one another is a foolishness which 'the world' does not admire or perhaps even tolerate.

3 ORDER AND ORGANIZATION IN THE ANGLICAN COMMUNION

1 NEW PROVINCES

Autonomous Provinces constitute the member Churches of the Anglican Communion. The creation of a new Province is therefore a matter which involves the whole family of Churches of the Communion. The terms of reference of the Anglican Consultative Council, approved by all the member Churches, include:

To advise on inter-Anglican, provincial, and diocesan relationships, including the division of provinces, the formation of new provinces and of regional councils, and the problems of extra-provincial dioceses.

At the first meeting of the ACC at Limuru in 1971 Resolution 21 was passed, describing the necessary marks of a Province, and requiring that, before the creation of a new Province, there should be consultation with the ACC or its Standing Committee for guidance and advice.

Three such proposals were before ACC 2 in Dublin:

(a) CONSEJO ANGLICANO SUD AMERICANO

The Council considered the proposed Constitution for an Anglican Council of South America (CASA) (see p. 42 below) an acceptable alternative to the traditional Province, and encouraged the dioceses of South America to persevere in the framing of a final constitution in order to bring CASA into being. The proposal was commended as a means of combining flexibility and authority while avoiding excessive centralization. It was seen as a means of giving identity to the Anglican Church in the area. Hope was expressed that the independent Province of Brazil would consider seriously its possible membership in CASA in order to preserve the unity of Anglican witness in South America. It further suggested that in the final Constitution special attention should be directed to:

(i) the development of a procedure which would involve both the diocese and CASA in the choice of bishops;
(ii) clarification of the role and functions of the continuing body to serve between the meetings of CASA;
(iii) provision for the clear relationship of diocesan constitutions to CASA.

Resolution 19   Anglican Council of South America

The Council recommends to the dioceses in South America and to the Province of Brazil that they should proceed with plans for the setting up of the Anglican Council of South America (CASA) after due attention to the points in the Report.

(b) COUNCIL OF THE EPISCOPAL CHURCH OF JERUSALEM AND THE MIDDLE EAST

The Council recommended without change the proposed Constitution for a Council of the Episcopal Church of Jerusalem and the Middle East, comprising the uniting dioceses of Jordan–Lebanon–Syria and Jerusalem, a new diocese of Cyprus and the Gulf, the diocese of Egypt, and the diocese of Iran.

The Council recognizes that a procedure of election within the Province of a bishop for the diocese of Jerusalem would supersede the present practice of the appointment from outside the Province of an Anglican Archbishop in Jerusalem. While acknowledging the special place of Jerusalem in the Christian world, the Council believes that the general principal that the Anglican Church in any place is represented by its elected diocesan bishop should also obtain in Jerusalem and the Middle East, the bishop's function being primarily as minister and pastor.

The association of the whole Anglican Communion with the city and Church of Jerusalem might be expressed by strengthening the system of appointing bishops from various parts of the world as episcopal canons of St George's Cathedral in Jerusalem. Under the chairmanship of the Bishop in Jerusalem they might also serve as an advisory body to the Dean and Chapter. In making this suggestion the Council is also mindful of the unique position of Jerusalem as a centre of pilgrimage, and the consequent role of St George's Cathedral.

Although it is not explicit in the draft Constitution, the Council understands and fully approves that the metropolitan authority of the proposed Council would be by delegation. This might best be set down on the following lines:

(a) by delegation from the Archbishop of Canterbury the Council of the Episcopal Church of Jerusalem and the Middle East (and no other body) shall have and exercise sole metropolitan authority including:

(i) To authorize the election of a bishop in any vacant diocese, to arrange for his consecration, and to give his licence;

(ii) To rescind a bishop's licence, constitutionally and on adequate canonical grounds;

(iii) To authorize the appointment and/or consecration of any assistant or non-diocesan bishop.

(b) (i) If the Council should decide to disband, metropolitan authority shall revert to the Archbishop of Canterbury.

(ii) If the Archbishop of Canterbury decides that the Council is no longer competent for its purposes, he may resume his jurisdiction.

The Council agrees that the diocese of the Sudan should separate from the Jerusalem Archbishopric with a view to becoming a separate Province.

Although the remaining dioceses which would form the new Council of Jerusalem and the Middle East have a small membership, the Council agrees that there would be the required minimum of four dioceses at the time of the inauguration of the proposed Council, and also considers that, if the particular circumstances of the Middle East made it desirable, there might be five dioceses.

The Council agrees that within the Constitution for the proposed Council there should be a particular Constitution for St George's College, Jerusalem.

Resolution 20 Council of Jerusalem and the Middle East

The Council recommends that the dioceses of the Jerusalem Archbishopric should inaugurate a Council as outlined in the Draft, taking into account the specific recommendations in this Report.

(c) DIOCESE OF THE SUDAN

The diocese of the Sudan, which has a membership of a quarter of a million, is at present part of the Jerusalem Archbishopric, and thus ultimately under the jurisdiction of the Archbishop of Canterbury. The diocese wishes to proceed to provincial status.

Resolution 21 The Sudan

The Council advises that the diocese of the Sudan should be authorized to revert to the sole jurisdiction of the Archbishop of Canterbury as an extra-provincial diocese, pending the establishment of the new Province of the Sudan.

(d) THE PROPOSED CONSTITUTION FOR THE PROVINCE OF MELANESIA

The Council received a draft Constitution for the creation of a Province of Melanesia. It stated that since this is a constitution based on traditional Anglican principles, the diocese of Melanesia should go forward with its plans to become a Province. It observed that there will be the minimum of four dioceses and it has confidence that the other requirements of Limuru Resolution 21 will be met. It noted further that in the Draft much of the Constitution is, in effect, in outline. The intention is that the outline should be filled in by the Province itself after its inauguration. However, the Council thinks that parts of the

Constitution should be more complete before the Province is inaugurated, particularly:

Article 3—'The Area of the Province'; diocesan boundaries should be specified.

Article 8—'The appointment of the Archbishop'.

Article 13—'The way in which the bishops are appointed'.

Article 18—'Church courts'.

The Council, recognizing the need for urgency, also believes that procedures and canonical requirements relating to both the creation of the four dioceses and the inauguration of the Province (Article 21) should now be worked out precisely.

The Council further recommends:

(i) A re-drafting of Article 1, 'Foundations which cannot be changed', probably in more traditional Anglican phraseology, to reduce possibilities of misinterpretation;

(ii) A re-drafting of Article 20 giving consideration to the advantages of distinguishing between articles that are of the Church's Constitution on the one hand, and canons or regulations on the other.

The Council draws attention to the following comments.

Because of the loneliness and isolation to which a small Province is liable, the Council recommends that the Church in Melanesia should seek opportunities to develop the fullest possible relationships with other dioceses and Churches in the southern Pacific, and particularly with the South Pacific Anglican Council. The Council is confident that the parent Church in New Zealand is aware of the role it might play in this context.

Resolution 22   Proposed Province of Melanesia

The Council recommends that the diocese of Melanesia and the Province of New Zealand proceed with plans for constituting a Province of Melanesia, and that when these are agreed to by the diocese and the General Synod of the Province, the Council recommends that the new Province may be formed.

(e)   PROLIFERATION OF PROVINCES

The consideration of all the above proposed constitutions, and information regarding discussions currently proceeding with a view to establishing provincial or conciliar structures—in Papua-New Guinea and the dioceses of Province IX of the Episcopal Church, USA, led the Council to observe that the proliferation of autonomous Provinces, small in size, numbers, or resources, should be avoided. It recommended that in some cases a form of conciliar organization to link dioceses scattered over a wide area would be preferable. It suggested that the time may well have come to scrutinize traditional Anglican structures, both provincial and conciliar, to see whether there are other models more appropriate to the Church's life in a world of increasing mobility and rapid change.

2 METROPOLITAN FUNCTIONS

(a) DIOCESE OF CUBA

The Council considered the isolated state of the diocese of Cuba. It appreciated the concern of the Primate of Canada that the Metropolitan Council for the diocese of Cuba, of which he is Chairman, is not succeeding in giving the diocese the support he is convinced it should have.

The Council believes that some action must be taken, and recommends that a meeting of the Metropolitan Council be arranged as soon as possible, together with three or four other people sympathetic to the situation of the diocese of Cuba, to devise effective means for its support.

(b) ISOLATED DIOCESES

The Council took cognizance of the fact that, from time to time, by reason of political and other circumstances, the need can arise for the provision of metropolitan functions for dioceses which become isolated from their former metropolitan authority. It therefore passed the following:

Resolution 23   Metropolitan Functions

The following proposal is submitted to the member Churches of the Anglican Communion for their approval:

In any case in which they are satisfied that the existing metropolitan provision for a diocese or group of dioceses can no longer operate, the President of the Anglican Consultative Council, in consultation with the Chairman and the Secretary General, is authorized to make the necessary provision for such metropolitan functions.

3 LITURGY

Limuru Resolution 26 requested that the Secretary General 'arrange for a report on liturgical matters to be made to the ACC in 1973'.

The Council received with gratitude the fine report by Canon Jasper and recommended that it be published in this Report (see chapter 6, pp. 70–86 below).

While expressing the feeling that a central liturgical commission is impracticable at the present time, the Council recommends continuing collaboration among the various Liturgical Commissions. It questions whether the problems connected with the provision of liturgies in acceptable modern English have been satisfactorily solved, and notes the difficulties involved in the translation, adaptation, and development of modern liturgies in other languages. It suggests that expert help should be given to member Churches which face these problems. It recognizes that within a common eucharistic structure the present tendency is towards variety and transience.

4 CHRISTIAN INITIATION

The Council noted that in a number of Churches, including the Church of England, the Anglican Church of Canada, and the Episcopal Church, USA, similar discussions are proceeding. Information regarding the progress of the work in Canada was available to the Council.

A document entitled *A Form for the Affirmation of Baptismal Vows with the Laying on of Hands by the Bishop, also called Confirmation* was received from the Episcopal Church, USA. The Council calls attention to the fact that the role of confirmation appears to be the often unrecognized focus of many of the problems arising in relation to Christian initiation. Questions are being raised regarding (*a*) the necessity of confirmation being performed by a bishop; (*b*) the usual necessity of confirmation for admission to Holy Communion; and (*c*) the association of confirmation with programmes of instruction.

The problem underlying these questions is that of the relation of confirmation to the basic sequence of Christian initiation. Current proposals for the revision of traditional Anglican procedures for the initiation of children embody two contrasting solutions of this problem. In some cases (e.g. the decision of the Canadian General Synod, 1971), confirmation is retained within the initiatory sequence, but as part of a single baptismal rite. In other cases confirmation is no longer treated as part of Christian initiation (in the fundamental sense of admission to communicant membership in the Church) but is viewed as a step in the maturing communicant's development. Both suggested procedures have one important common factor, namely the closing of the gap between baptism and first communion; and their effect on our practice and basic understanding of initiation and church membership would in most respects be identical. The two proposals differ, however, both in their sacramental theology of confirmation and in certain implications for pastoral practice (e.g. concerning the weight to be given to a single public act of renewal or affirmation of baptismal vows).

35

The Council therefore suggests that the underlying problem merits further study, including a serious exchange of views among the member Churches (see also Appendix 2, pp. 43–6 below).

Resolution 24   Information on Christian Initiation

The Secretary General is asked to circulate to member Churches information regarding the studies on Christian Initiation mentioned in the Report, and similar studies from other Churches, indicating how each may be obtained.

5 POLYGAMY AND MONOGAMY

The Council received the excellent volume *Christian Marriage in Africa* by Adrian Hastings, a book which was commissioned by the Archbishops of Cape Town, Central Africa, Kenya, Tanzania, and Uganda. The Council commends this book to the Churches for study and draws attention to Fr Hastings' enumeration of four different views of polygamy which Christians might hold (p. 73):

(*a*) Polygamy is simply a sin, comparable with adultery.

(*b*) Polygamy is an inferior form of marriage, not sinful where it is the custom but always unacceptable for Christians.

(*c*) Polygamy is a form of marriage less satisfactory than monogamy and one which cannot do justice to the full spirit of Christian marriage, but in certain circumstances individual Christians can still put up with it, as they put up with slavery, dictatorial government, and much else.

(*d*) Polygamy is one form of marriage, monogamy another. Each has its advantages and disadvantages: they are appropriate to different types of society. It is not the task of the Church to make any absolute judgement between them.

Of the above, Fr Hastings favoured position (*c*).

Fr Hastings also says:

When Christians enter marriage, they should do so conscious that it is a sacrament both of Christian anthropology and of Christian redemption: by its very shape, its monogamous and indissoluble character, it bears witness both to what man is and to what the covenant is, the relationship of Christ and his Church. If one becomes a Christian, this is part of the gospel one accepts and therefore it is not an open question for one then to enter into a polygamous marriage. For a married person marriage stands very close to the core of being a Christian, and this means that—in so far as it now depends upon one—it must be made a witness both by its structures and by its spirit to the Christian vision of man and of Christ (pp. 75–6).

The Council also considered the recommendations made by the All Africa Conference of Churches at Ibadan in 1958.

Resolution 25   Polygamy

The Council recommends to the Churches:

(*a*) Fr Adrian Hastings' book *Christian Marriage in Africa;*

(*b*) that in the case of the conversion of a pagan polygamist, he should be received into the Church with his believing wives and children, provided that this should only be done in suitable cases with the willing consent of the local Christian community, and only within a context where the Church's teaching on monogamy is strictly recognized;

(*c*) that they should actively pursue educational policies on the nature and discipline of Christian marriage.

In connection with the above Resolution the Council also considered the position of individual Christians who become polygamists, and suggested there might be some cases in which special consideration should be given.

6   MINISTRY

The Council discussed a wide range of issues concerning Christian Ministry but, because of the complexity of the questions, it found itself unable to say anything of sufficient depth or quality to report to the member Churches. The Council therefore agreed to devote a major portion of time to this subject at the meeting of the Council in 1975, with sufficient time in the agenda for adequate study and discussion.

It was thought that the question of the ordination of women should also form part of this total study of Ministry. In relation to this there was a strong request for a study of the relative status of the male and female principle and the symbolic authority they exercise upon our understanding of the nature of God and of leadership roles in Church and society.

7   THE ORDINATION OF WOMEN TO THE PRIESTHOOD

There is no more pressing and perplexing problem of ministry than that of the ordination of women to the priesthood. In recent years, notably for the last decade, an increasing number of Provinces and dioceses have given more time and attention to this question. This resulted at Limuru in the adoption of Resolution 28, reprinted below. Before considering this, however, it is important to remind ourselves of the limitations of the Anglican Consultative Council in what it may and may not do.

As its name states, the Council is a *Consultative* body. It does not legislate. It can inform members of each other's actions and can advise any Church on specific matters of concern. It is not possible for the Council to adopt any resolution which would force any member Church to ordain women, or to refuse to do so. It does not have this power. It does not wish to have it.

(a) BACKGROUND OF THE LIMURU ACTION

The 1968 Lambeth Conference asked all the Anglican Churches to study the ordination of women to the priesthood and to report their findings to the newly forming ACC. At the date of the first meeting, February 1971, there were eight such Churches which had begun to act on the Lambeth request, but none had sent in its results. Thus the Council might reasonably have postponed any statement until its 1973 meeting, except that the Bishop of Hong Kong (the Right Reverend Gilbert Baker) had asked advice on what course to follow, since his diocesan synod had approved in principle the ordination of women to the priesthood.

This specific request came from the very diocese whose earlier bishop, the Right Reverend R. O. Hall, during the war in 1944 had, at a time when one of its churches in the neighbouring island of Macao had no priest, ordained a woman. The action was not supported by Lambeth 1948 and there had been no such ordination since. But Hong Kong was by no means the only place where the question was important. The eight Churches which had begun to act on the Lambeth request are indicative of that. Position papers, study guides, scholarly essays on biblical and theological background, and articles for and against in the church press, were clear evidence that interest, even concern, was widespread. But it was the request from Hong Kong that precipitated the action indicated in Limuru Resolution 28, here reprinted in full:

(a) Many of the Churches of the Anglican Communion regard the question of ordination of women to the priesthood as an urgent matter. We therefore call on all Churches of the Anglican Communion to give their consideration to this subject as requested by LCR 35 and to express their views in time for consideration by the Anglican Consultative Council in 1973.

(b) In reply to the request of the Council of the Church of South-East Asia, this Council advises the Bishop of Hong Kong, acting with the approval of his Synod, and any other bishop of the Anglican Communion acting with the approval of his Province, that, if he decides to ordain women to the priesthood, his action will be acceptable to this Council; and that this Council will use its good offices to encourage all Provinces of the Anglican Communion to continue in communion with these dioceses.   *Carried by 24 votes to 22*

(c) In the terms of LCR 36, the Secretary General is asked to request the metropolitans and primates of the Churches of the Anglican Communion to consult with other Churches in their area in the matter of ordination of women and to report to him in time for the next meeting of the Anglican Consultative Council (Limuru Report, pp. 38–9).

Resolution 28 offers a positive decision, whilst at the same time admitting the limits of the Council's power to decide on such a question. The Council had been informed that provinces were still studying the question, and would have acted improperly if it had either prejudged their findings or taken upon itself to decide questions which lay within their competence. But, as member after member made clear in the debate, it would be still more improper to postpone whatever decision lay within the power of the Council ... The Holy Spirit ... could also be expected to speak through the Anglican Churches when they reflected on the resolution and made known their views (Limuru Report, pp. 34–5).

(b) ACTION SINCE LIMURU

As was widely reported in both church and secular press throughout the world, the Bishop of Hong Kong on Advent Sunday, 1971, ordained to the priesthood the Reverend Jane Hwang and the Reverend Joyce Bennett, both of whom had served for several years in the diocese of Hong Kong, and were widely known and respected by the clergy and laity of the diocese. There *are*, therefore, two women priests in the Anglican Communion.

No Church or Province has ceased to be in communion with the diocese of Hong Kong. This is not to say that all of them approve the action taken. In fairness it must be said, however, that remaining in communion indicates that the other Churches and Provinces respect the right of Hong Kong to its action, in the light of Limuru Resolution 28.

A number of Churches and Provinces have prepared reports or papers on the Ordination of Women to the Priesthood. These are from the Church of England, the Church in Wales, the Church of the Province of New Zealand, the Church of the Province of South Africa, and the Protestant Episcopal Church in the USA. The Church of England in Australia and the Anglican Church of Canada have both carried out similar studies. These reports represent an enormous investment of time and effort, and bear witness to the seriousness with which the matter of the Ordination of Women to the Priesthood is regarded. Further, it is hard to imagine *any* aspect of this subject which has not been examined by competent scholars, committees, and boards. The report made to the General Synod of the Church of England is particularly recommended for study. It is an eighty-seven page document, admirably indexed and annotated, and containing information and references not otherwise easily assembled.

The present position with regard to the Ordination of Women indicates clearly that there has been considerable movement since

Limuru 1971. A tidy account is not easy because of the varied wording of the resolutions adopted by different Churches, briefly reported here under four headings:

(a) Ordination of women approved and women ordained to the priesthood:
The diocese of *Hong Kong*.

(b) Ordination of women approved in principle:

(i) The Church of the Province of *Burma:* 'this Council accepts on principle the ordination of women to the priesthood and agrees to its introduction when circumstances so require it'.
(ii) The Church of the Province of *New Zealand:* 'that the General Synod approves in principle of the Ordination of Women to the Priesthood'. The Synod further agreed to take no action with regard to the ordination of women to the priesthood until there is further advice from the ACC in 1973.
(iii) The Anglican Church of *Canada:* 'that this General Synod accept the principle of the Ordination of Women to the Priesthood, that this decision be communicated to the ACC, and that implementation not take place until the House of Bishops has worked out a pattern for the Canadian Church that would include an educational process for the Church' (May 1973).

(e) Preliminary actions taken, final action pending:

(i) Church of *England:* the Report of the Advisory Council for the Church's Ministry on the Ordination of Women to the Priesthood has been discussed in both the Convocations of York and Canterbury. The Synod, meeting in July 1973, accepted the recommendations of its Standing Committee that the Report be referred to dioceses for study and discussion. It is believed that this will take eighteen to twenty-four months after which it will come before the General Synod for a formal decision.
(ii) Church in *Wales:* the Report of the Doctrinal Commission has been referred to the dioceses for study, looking towards action at a future date.
(iii) *USA:* in November 1972 the House of Bishops voted that it was the mind of the house that women should be ordained to the priesthood and episcopate (in favour 74, against 61, abstentions 5). It was further voted to recommend that the General Convention in October 1973 should adopt canons to enable the ordination of women to the priesthood.
(iv) The Church of England in *Australia:* the General Synod received in May 1973 a Report on the question by the Commission on Doctrine and has referred the Report to the dioceses for study.

(*d*) Negative action taken:

(i) The *South Pacific* Anglican Council reported that most of its people are not yet ready to accept women priests.

(ii) *Central Africa* reported that it would not be opportune at the time to proceed with any proposal. Study by each diocese, however, has been recommended.

The Council notes a somewhat anomalous situation in which Churches report that they are waiting to see what consensus is developing in the Anglican Communion, or that they are waiting for further action by this Council meeting in Dublin. This deprives us of their contribution to the very consensus they seek, and tends to discourage further action by this Council. We repeat our assurance to the member Churches, Provinces, Councils, and extra-provincial dioceses, that the decision on the ordination of women to the priesthood is theirs alone.

The Council is aware that it has a leadership role and that more than one member Church expects further *action* by this body. It therefore adopts the following *statements* as the mind of the Council:

(i) The Council agrees to recommend once more that, where any autonomous Province of the Anglican Communion decides to ordain women to the priesthood, this should not cause any break in communion in our Anglican family.

Carried.   *In favour 50, against 2, abstentions 3*

(ii) The Council recognizes that any firm decision on the ordination of women to the priesthood will have important ecumenical repercussions, which need to be taken into account; but this consideration should not be decisive. The Churches of the Anglican Communion must make their own decision.

Carried.   *In favour 54, against 1, abstentions nil.*

(iii) The Churches, Provinces and extra-provincial dioceses which have not yet responded to the Secretary General in terms of Limuru Resolution 28(*a*) and (*c*) are again urged to do so, in order that a wider consensus of opinion may be obtained for further deliberation at ACC 3 in Perth in 1975.

Carried.   *In favour 54, against 1, abstentions nil.*

Note: Attention is drawn to Section 6 on Ministry (p. 37 above).

The form of statement (i), above, on which the Council voted at the session on the evening of Thursday 26 July had the words 'break in fellowship' instead of 'break in communion'. At the beginning of the session on Friday 27 July, the change to the word 'communion' was agreed in order to bring the resolution into line with Limuru Resolution

28 (*b*), which the Council agreed had been its understanding during the debate. The Right Reverend Paul Burrough (Bishop of Mashonaland) then made the following protest:

'I wish formally to protest that in a motion which had been in the hands of the Council for 24 hours, and debated for nearly 4 hours, a material alteration of the wording of the motion should have been made on the morning after the motion had been voted upon.'

APPENDIX 1

THE ANGLICAN COUNCIL OF SOUTH AMERICA (CASA)

The Draft Constitution

The draft Constitution is for a Council which will relate together the eleven Anglican dioceses in South America. This first draft originates from a Consultation of representatives from all the dioceses which met in Lima, Peru, in March 1973. The draft, which is still partly in outline only, is at present under discussion in the dioceses and is under revision.

Background

The Anglican Church in South America has a total communicant membership of fewer than 30,000, spread over the whole continent. Four dioceses form the autonomous Province of Brazil, two (Colombia and Ecuador) are missionary dioceses of the Episcopal Church, USA, one (Venezuela) is responsible to the Province of the West Indies, and the other four (Argentina, Chile, Northern Argentina, and Paraguay) are extra-provincial dioceses under the jurisdiction of the Archbishop of Canterbury. The dioceses have different histories and have had virtually no general common life or identity.

The Lima Consultation considered that an Anglican Province of the traditional style was inappropriate. For so large an area, and for so many countries, a more flexible and less centralized structure was sought, which nevertheless should include a body with some real authority. The Council as outlined in the draft is designed to meet this requirement.

The Council

The distinctive feature of the proposed Council is that it would have metropolitan functions *delegated* to it by the present metropolitan authorities. (Whether or not the Province of Brazil would similarly delegate authority, or simply have representation on the Council, is still under discussion.) The Council's exercise of the delegated metropolitan functions is described as follows in the Draft Constitution:

Metropolitan functions

A. By delegation from several present Metropolitan authorities (Canterbury, Brazil, USA, West Indies), the Council (and no other body) shall have sole authority:

(i) To authorize the election of a Bishop in any vacant diocese, to arrange for his consecration, and to give his licence.

(ii) A Bishop's licence may be rescinded, on adequate canonical grounds, by a three-quarter majority vote of the diocesan bishops of CASA assembled together. (Note: At one of its first meetings CASA shall determine a procedure for appeal by a Bishop against deprivation of his licence.) When the licence is officially rescinded the diocese shall be declared vacant.

(iii) To authorize the appointment and/or consecration of any assistant or non-diocesan Bishop. (Probably CASA shall also have the authority to authorize the creation of any new diocese in South America.)

B. Dioceses not in a Province in South America shall, at least for the time being, continue to operate under their present canons and regulations, and (by delegation of authority from the several present metropolitan authorities) dioceses shall be responsible for so doing to CASA.

Each diocese shall have authority to change its regulations and canons, but a diocese should seek the advice and counsel of CASA before making any radical departure from generally accepted Anglican forms and practices.

Dioceses in a Province in South America continue subject to the canons and regulations of that Province and to its Provincial Synod.

These provisions are a part of the flexibility appropriate to so wide and diverse an area. Also, should circumstances or political situations make it desirable, the delegated metropolitan jurisdiction in respect of a diocese of the Council could be resumed by the original Metropolitan; a procedure thus described in the Draft Constitution:

The Disbandment of CASA

(a) If CASA should decide to disband, Metropolitan authority delegated to it shall revert to the respective original Metropolitan authorities.

(b) If any original Metropolitan authority decides that CASA is no longer competent for its purposes that Authority may resume its jurisdiction.

It is proposed that membership of the Council should include clergy and laity as well as bishops, and that the Council should meet at least every three years.

APPENDIX 2

MEMORANDUM ON CONFIRMATION: THE BASIC ISSUE

BY PROFESSOR EUGENE FAIRWEATHER, ANGLICAN CHURCH OF CANADA

After a speech by Professor Fairweather the Council invited him to write this Memorandum expressing his own views.

The report of Section 3 (pp. 35–6 above) asserts that confirmation is 'the often unrecognized focus' of many problems connected with Christian initiation. After identifying certain specific questions, it goes on to suggest that the underlying problem may be defined as 'the relation of confirmation to the basic sequence of Christian initiation.' What follows is my personal attempt to develop this diagnosis of our situation.

To begin with, I must say something about the historical background of our problems. It is indisputable that, in the common practice of the early Church, initiation (whether of adults or of children) led directly to participation in the eucharist, the central corporate act of the worshipping community. The essential relationship between incorporation into the body and sharing in the offering of the body, between the baptismal dying and rising with Christ and the eucharistic memorial of his death and resurrection, was thus clearly expressed. This sacramental pattern has remained substantially unchanged in the practice of the Eastern Churches. In the medieval West, however, historical circumstances led to a division of the earlier single rite of initiation into baptism, ordinarily administered by a priest, and confirmation, administered by a bishop. The most conspicuous result of this development was the postponement of first communion, in the case of children, for some years after baptism—a practice which has tended to obscure the essential unity of initiation and eucharist, of church membership and sacramental communion.

The role of confirmation in perpetuating the separation between initiation and eucharist has varied from Church to Church in the post-medieval West. It has been least important in the Roman Catholic Church, where the further development of medieval trends in both practice and theology has led to a widespread removal of confirmation from its place in the traditional initiatory sequence and to its reinterpretation as a sacrament of Christian maturity. It has been much more significant in the Lutheran and Reformed traditions, where a course of intensive instruction, culminating in a rite of confirmation, has been required of those baptized in infancy as a condition of communicant membership. (The fact that in these traditions confirmation is not interpreted sacramentally has not affected its practical importance as a step between infant baptism and the eucharist.) Perhaps the role of confirmation has been most important in Anglicanism, where a persistent emphasis on confirmation as the climax of preparation for communion has been more and more widely complemented by an insistence on the sacramental meaning of confirmation as the completion of baptism.

In recent years radical criticism of our traditional pattern has become widespread in the Anglican Communion. The weightiest theological factor in such criticism has been a renewed awareness of the essential link between initiation and eucharist, in the context of a fresh appreciation of the Church as eucharistic community. To many of us it now seems well-nigh intolerable that incorporation into the Church through baptism should not lead directly to a sharing in the central act of the Church's worship and life. For this and other reasons, theological, pastoral, and ecumenical, the various Anglican Churches are being urged to undertake a drastic reform of their liturgical and pastoral practice of Christian initiation.

It is obvious that confirmation, as ordinarily practised and interpreted among Anglicans, is a major obstacle to such a reform. For Anglican children confirmation, treated as a separate sacramental rite and administered only after extended instruction and a renewal of baptismal vows, stands between the basic act of Christian initiation and admission to the privilege of communion. If an adequate reform is to be carried out and the essential orientation of baptism to the eucharist is to be made plain, confirmation as we have known it must surely go. But just how are we to reform this particular element in our tradition?

Two contrasting answers to this question are emerging in current Anglican proposals.

(a) On the one hand, a return to the common practice of the Church in the age of the church fathers and the ecumenical councils is being urged. That is to say, it is proposed that what we now know as the sacramental act of confirmation should be retracted into a single rite of initiation, consisting of baptism in water followed by the laying on of hands and/or anointing with chrism. This single rite would admit the recipient directly to the eucharistic table. Patterns of Christian education would be radically reshaped, to emphasize the nurture of the young in full communicant life.

(b) On the other hand, a removal of any sacramental act of initiation other than baptism in water is being proposed. If confirmation (or something like it) were retained, it would cease to be a properly initiatory rite at all and become an act of commissioning or blessing for adult Christian responsibility, accompanied by a solemn affirmation or renewal of baptismal vows. Patterns of Christian education would be radically altered, as in proposal (a).

It is clear that either proposal, if accepted, would meet the main theological requirement which I have stated in this paper. In either case the gap between baptism and eucharist would be closed and the present scandal of a class of apparently half-initiated Christians would be abolished. At the point where reform is most urgently needed, then, the two proposals would have the same effect. There are, nevertheless, some good grounds for preferring proposal (a). The following, at least, should be mentioned here.

1. Proposal (a) takes seriously the testimony of the early Christian tradition, according to which the full sacramental rite of initiation includes imposition of hands and/or unction as well as baptism in water. As we have seen, this tradition is maintained in the Eastern Churches and reflected, though with more or less serious distortion, in the West. It is not self-evident that it can simply be dismissed as a guide to the practice and understanding of Christian initiation. (On this ground the English *Ely Report* seems to me to be open to serious criticism.)

2. Proposal (a) retains the sacramental gesture of confirmation as part of

the total sacramental sign of initiation, without separating confirmation from baptism, and therefore without introducing the puzzling (and perhaps insoluble) Western problem of the theological interpretation of confirmation as a separate sacrament. (In my view, this puzzle is not solved even by the drastic expedient of transferring confirmation from the initiatory sequence to another context. On the contrary, the further confirmation is removed from baptism, the stronger the theological temptation must be to abolish it altogether, as something impossible to explain without eroding the unique significance of the baptismal rite.)

3. Proposal (*a*) allows us to treat the renewal of baptismal vows more flexibly and adequately. It is both theologically and pastorally desirable to contrast the once-for-all act of God in the sacramental action of Christian initiation with the ongoing process of appropriation, punctuated by repeated acts of reaffirmation and renewed commitment. To focus attention on a single act of renewal, especially if it is linked with confirmation as the sacrament of Christian maturity, is to risk blurring this contrast. Proposal (*a*) excludes this danger by holding uncompromisingly to a single sacramental rite which fully incorporates those who share it into the priestly and apostolic community, but whose effects are to be realized in a lifelong process.

It may be useful to append a note on the ecumenical consequences of proposal (*a*). Some Anglicans fear that its adoption would call into question the status of Christians initiated by water-baptism alone and would thus impede the movement towards wider intercommunion. I suggest that, while we wait hopefully for other Churches to find the same path to renewal, we may well meet the anticipated difficulty by a generous application of the principle of 'economy'. In any case, as the Anglican Consultative Council has remarked in another context, the Anglican Churches must make their own decision on matters of internal reform.

4 MISSION AND EVANGELISM

Part A: Dialogue, Evangelism, and Renewal

Introduction:
The Church's task in evangelism has to be related to its cultural and social context, and has to take account of the nature of its own structures and the effectiveness of its instruments. Following Bangkok 1973 we have given attention to the three main issues raised in that Report, in an attempt to relate its findings to the task of the Anglican Communion and the mission of God in the world today.

We wish to highlight three things as particularly relevant to the task of evangelism. The first is the need for dialogue, not only with Christians of other Churches, but also with people of other faiths or none. 'Dialogue will not be simply another form of evangelism' (Limuru, p. 44). It is to help those who engage in it to perceive the needs and spiritual resources of the other, so that thereby both may be drawn closer to the truth as it is in Jesus. The second is the fact that the gospel is obscured for people today as much as at any time by the injustice of social and political structures, for which Christians have varying degrees of responsibility. In these circumstances the gospel cannot be preached without action by Christians to change the situation where this can be done wisely and effectively. The third is that without the renewal of the Church both spiritually and structurally its evangelism cannot be effective.

1 *Peoples of Other Religions and Cultures*
The mission of the Church has to be carried on among people of other faiths, and among the many who profess no religious faith, whether it be by conscious rejection of what they have inherited, or by growing into a pattern of life to which the whole dimension of the spiritual seems irrelevant. It has also to be carried on in cultures other than that of the Semitic, Mediterranean, and Western background.

Our faith is in God the Creator of all, and we therefore expect to find him at work among all people of his creating. We know from our experience of God-in-Christ, that he wills to be the Fulfiller and Redeemer of all. We start out on God's mission to the world, grateful for what he has done for us in Christ, and confident in his purpose of love to unite all people in a world community based on justice, freedom, and love. Christians are therefore called to meet their fellow men in a spirit of genuine respect, eager to hear of their religious experience, and to study the effects of it in character, daily living, and community spirit, as well as in its expression in cultural life. They must also be willing to learn why religion seems to others to be irrelevant. We shall not unthinkingly assume that we have nothing to learn or receive from others, but be ready to listen and learn as well as share our faith and experience. We shall want to be as loving, humble, and serving as our Lord, both as individuals and in our corporate fellowship in his Church.

The Church in each land has a distinctive mission, related to the traditional religion and culture of the people of that country. In some areas of the world there are religions with a long, recorded history, with written scriptures and commentaries, with some form of ministry and traditional patterns of worship. In other countries there are people, with little in the way of written records, but with a consciousness of the spiritual world, expressed in all the personal, family, tribal, and community happenings of life, a dependence on nature, the customs of sacrifices, and a solidarity with ancestors. Christians have tended to write off this 'primal' religion as full of fear and superstition, and there is indeed both the need and the opportunity for the cleansing, saving, sanctifying grace of our Lord Jesus Christ; but it is for those who practise it an authentic form of religious experience. In many countries there is a belief in a Supreme God who lives far removed from men, who is thought of as being reached through the ancestors, and persuaded not to punish but to bless. In all these traditions we can see how Christ would come as Saviour, Sanctifier, and Fulfiller.

Christians may study with interest and reverence the religious faith and practices of other men. There is a place for scholarly dialogue to understand more deeply, for the pastor to bring the grace of God, for the evangelist to relate the gospel to what people already have, for Christians to have fellowship with those of other faiths in their daily lives.

In this understanding of other faiths there will be opportunity for forms of Christian worship which express the sanctified experience of the past in ways meaningful and congenial to each particular culture. Church buildings will not always copy those of the West, but be recognizable as places connected with prayer and worship of an indigenous character. Hymns will come out of spiritual experience and not be just translations, while music may start from folklore tunes and go on to new compositions.

We are critical of the liturgies being produced by different Churches of the Anglican Communion as being mainly rearrangements of 1662 and Series 2 of the Church of England. We hope that consideration might be given to the possible inclusion of elements of worship from the traditional religion of the country where the Church carries on its mission.

We also encourage a study of the spirituality in other religions, particularly methods of silence, meditation, and contemplation, which are attracting the attention of many young people.

48

A further suggestion is the study of forms of ministry in other religions which might result in some new understanding of the care of people, the conduct of worship, the development of community, and the preparation for the future life.

We are convinced that our starting point is God-in-Christ, and that, because we believe that Christ is the Light of the World, we must gladly recognize any light wherever we find it. Our confidence is that as we go out to the world we shall discover more of the Living Christ at work. We acknowledge in penitence that as individuals and Churches we need to grow more Christlike in love, holiness, and servanthood, and that our approach to men of other faiths and our dialogue with them will be more acceptable and effective if we have previously carried out this exercise with our fellow-Christians. When we have found unity with them, we shall be the better prepared to work for the unity of all men in the love of God, who has shown himself so movingly and so compellingly in Jesus the Christ.

2 *The Society in which We Live*

Evangelization has to take into account the social structures within which and to which the gospel is being preached, as well as the structures of the Church from which it stems.

(*a*) Politically restrictive situations. Where the Church cannot speak out on issues of the time it still has the duty of caring for the people, thus demonstrating both a personal and social ministry. While sometimes the Church will have to suffer in silence it must, where it is possible, speak out on political issues. Where it is unwise for individuals to do so, the Christian viewpoint can sometimes be brought to those in authority by the joint action of groups of clergy and people. Conversely, it is recognized that the Church has opportunities in many situations to work *with* Governments in the promotion of a just society.

1973 is the twenty-fifth anniversary of the United Nations Declaration of Human Rights. The Church in its evangelistic role in society should remind Governments of the importance of this Declaration, especially in countries where people are being degraded and dehumanized. In the eyes of God all men are equal, but the actions of Governments in many parts of the world deny this. The duty of the Church is to be a catalyst for change by all possible and practical means.

(*b*) Apathy of affluence. It is tempting to think that the only place where the Church is in conflict is where it is in opposition to political ideologies, but there are also situations of affluence where apathy is the greatest enemy, and can so easily dull a sense of mission and allow the Church to be comfortable. These are most often the situations in which the Church has ceased to appear relevant to a new generation. In such situations, the Church must ask itself some searching questions;

for example, Why are we so comfortable when there are so many evils and apportunities to face? Is our very organization a structure which inhibits a real demonstration of the gospel? Does our complacent, self-preserving concern for the things of the past and for our own personal salvation prevent Christ from working through us?

Churches are called on to consider their resources and their use of them. This consideration should include a realistic assessment of whether the resources themselves are inhibiting the true ministry of the Church which is the proclamation both of a personal and a social gospel. We need to consider the most effective use of our church buildings, by sharing them with other denominations; possibly allowing people of other faiths to use them, and using them in addition for other purposes besides that of worship. The continuing construction of denominational and one-purpose buildings should be carefully scrutinized.

Apathy is a *group* sickness; personal, individual involvement is the way to overcome this. Parishes and schools should indicate and implement the exchange between countries of people of all ages and social classes, not necessarily in 'church' areas but in hospitals, schools, industry, labouring, and such cultural exchanges as are already operative in some parts of the world.

(c) The parish today. Is the parish church a social club for leisure time, a hospital, a protective insurance society? Or is it a place where a community comes together for worship, to give and to receive, and then to go into the world renewed for action? The Church's mission also extends outside the traditional limits within which we have sometimes tried to confine it.

Mission involves a going out into such fields as industry, medicine, labour, the arts, ecology, population problems, changing moral standards. The Church in order that all men 'may have life and have it more abundantly' must claim for them dignity, compassion, love, and tolerance. For this it must use the specialized knowledge and skills of the laity just as much as of the clergy, both inside the church building and beyond. Christian laity, in their households, their work and leisure, must exercise a full responsibility both as citizens and as Christians in a spirit of love, of humility, and of service, and in co-operation with men of good will everywhere.

There is today an awakening sympathy with the ideals of the religious community life. Its rejection of the values of a decadent society and the emphasis on spiritual awareness and interdependence is felt to have much in common with the idea of an 'alternative society'.

The Church must take the initiative, especially in newly developing residential and industrial areas, to aid the formation of new Christian communities in both the social and spiritual sense.

We are conscious that we have not been able to grapple with the decline of faith in the modern world or with the loss of consciousness of the spiritual dimension of life. Nor have we had time to think of dialogue with the atheist or agnostic, or with the Marxist. These are questions which concern people of all ages. We urge that such dialogue be initiated in each Church and shared with other Churches through the Secretary General.

3 *The Need to be Renewed for Effective Evangelism*

Evangelism includes the sharing with other people in a grateful, humble, and loving way what we have received through Jesus Christ: the knowledge of God, especially as seen in the love of the cross and in the power of the resurrection; the assurance of God's forgiveness of our sins, and of his grace to meet all the difficulties, temptations, adventures, and opportunities of life; and the assurance of a quality of life which physical death cannot destroy. When these benefits of grace and salvation are received through Jesus Christ and embodied in loving and saintly lives, people begin to see him in us, both as individuals and in the corporate life of each congregation.

For the renewal of spiritual life God is still using the traditional means of grace—prayer and sacrament, Scripture and meditation. He meets with those who come to him in these ways, and in and through them he works the true renewal which has its outlet in mission and evangelism. But if 'all the people of God' are to be 'equipped for ministry', they need to wait upon God that they may receive from him his own concern and love for the world; and their experience of this they need to share with one another. They need to expose themselves to what God is saying not only through Scripture, but also through the contemporary situation. Liturgical worship needs supplementing by more informal gatherings, where there may be a sharing of constraints and concerns which Christ lays on *every* member of his Body. The laity, whose daily work is in the world, are thus the principal means by which God takes action in that world. They should therefore become the means by which he sensitizes the Church to the world and its needs, and his mission to it in that local situation. Where there are gatherings of such a size that members are enabled to participate freely, there is opportunity to share, not only in prayer and Bible study, but also in opening up together what God is saying in the life and experience of each. The Holy Spirit uses the experience of each to speak to all, and there arise new matters for prayer and study, new dedication to service, and new programmes for mission.

Bangkok spoke of Church growth 'as being at the same time (i) the numerical growth of the Church, (ii) the development of a new man in every person; and (iii) the rooting of Christians' faith in local realities and their commitment to society'.

(i) 'The numerical growth of the Church.' We are still commissioned to go to all the world. Each Church should be planning that the gospel should be spoken to this generation in language and categories that they can hear and understand. The resources of the older Churches should be shared with those Churches whose task is too great for them to manage alone. On the other hand, the witness of members from the younger Churches may often help the older in the evangelization of those who have grown up familiar with the gospel but unchallenged by it.

Every congregation ought to review year by year its whole programme of mission and evangelism in its own neighbourhood and of its share in the world-wide commission.

(ii) 'The development of the new man in each person.' Growth is to be measured in the maturing of each person so that he is able to do God's work. All programmes of teaching and training should aim at service and witness and not merely an intellectual or pietistic goal. It must be emphasized that service here is not thought of as merely service to the Church but service to God in the world. This service may be in evangelism; it may also be in such worlds as industry, politics, sport, and suburban life. Teaching such as preparation for confirmation should not be merely of certain truths in a way which inclines to belief, or inculcates pious practice and life, but which prepares the candidate to be the man through whom God can work, 'in that state of life unto which it shall please God to call him'.

(iii) 'The rooting of Christians' faith in local realities and in their commitment to society.' The roots of faith are in God who is a God who reveals himself in history and in mission to the world. Any faith in such a God must result in sharing in his action and his mission.

Faith must continually be renewed through prayer and God's revelation of himself in Scripture. Those who are rooted in God must spread out into the realities of their society in two ways: to men and women as persons who need renewal through reconciliation to God and re-making by his Spirit; and to structures of society which must be re-made to bring men into right relationships to each other as individuals and in groups. The work of the renewal of men and women through reconciliation should be done in fellowship with all who have been reconciled in Christ. The renewal of structures may be done in fellowship with any who share with Christians the desire to see a better order for any part of creation. Their desire for what is just and true is a God-given desire, and may be regarded as a desire for his 'kingly rule'. It is rooted in Scripture but it is also found in many who do not acknowledge God, and therefore we can work with them for such renewal.

Resolution 26   Mission and Evangelism

In the light of the report on Mission and Evangelism the Council challenges anew the Church to embark on a prayerful, urgent, and realistic review of its role in all areas of society, and calls upon member Churches to set up or refer to appropriate committees, representative of all concerned, with a view to initiating action to recognize and remedy the deficiencies of the Church's work and witness, so that it may the better discharge its responsibilities to the whole community.

Part B: Concerning Mutual Responsibility and Interdependence in the Body of Christ (MRI)

INTRODUCTION

1   *One Mission*

The missionary task of the Church continues to be that of reconciling man to God, man to man, and man to his environment. The oneness of the missionary task throughout the world has been emphasized in recent years in all parts of the Christian Church. The emergence everywhere of autonomous churches in independent nations has challenged our inherited idea of mission as a movement from 'Christendom' in the West to the 'non-Christian' world. In its place has come the conviction that there is but one mission in all the world, and that this one mission is shared by the world-wide Christian community. The responsibility for mission in any place belongs *primarily* to the church in that place. However, the universality of the gospel and the oneness of God's mission mean also that this mission must be shared in each and every place with fellow-Christians from each and every part of the world with their distinctive insights and contributions. If we once acted as though there were only givers who had nothing to receive and receivers who had nothing to give, the oneness of the missionary task must now make us all both givers and receivers.

2   *Directory of Projects*

The MRI Directory of Projects was begun after Toronto 1963. The churches have submitted requests in the form of projects, and these have been compiled in the ACC office and circulated to all member churches for support.

The planning and sharing of information related to the MRI Directory of Projects has contributed to the development of a new approach to co-operation in mission within the Anglican Communion. It has, for example, encouraged planning on a regional as well as a diocesan basis, and it has been a source of information leading to new and significant interrelationships between churches. The MRI

53

concept has, however, been too largely identified with the Directory of Projects, and this in turn has led to a 'shopping list' mentality.

The Directory has become increasingly less effective both as a means of planning and as a means of support, and the newly published statistics on Membership, Manpower, and Money show that support of MRI projects accounts for only about 4 % of the total funds received by dioceses from outside sources. The new styles of co-operative partnership set out in Section B (below) are designed to overcome the weaknesses of the Directory system.

3 *Partnership in Mission*

Limuru stated that 'Missionary societies are beginning to see their programmes in relation to each other'. This development received further impetus at a meeting of representatives of missionary agencies in Greenwich, Connecticut, in 1972, when the following *aide-memoire* was drawn up:

(i) We are committed to an increasing effort to consult with each other in order to co-ordinate grants, personnel support, service projects, and our strategic planning. We make this commitment to each other in the conviction that mutual responsibility and interdependence requires of us—and we believe of other missionary societies as well—that we support the growing partnership of dioceses and Provinces throughout the Anglican Communion, and ecumenical collaboration, with an equal partnership and collaboration on the part of the missionary societies.

(ii) We believe the time requires of us that we work increasingly with Provinces and Regional Councils or other similar structures. The need is to support inter-diocesan planning for mission and to develop co-operative rather than unilateral structures for planning and priority decision-making in and for the areas. It is necessary for our societies to change previous patterns of operation in order to support the growing capacity for planning and decision-making on a Provincial or Regional Council basis in the Communion. There are national, geographical, cultural, historical, and other practical problems which must be resolved in consultation with all involved. But it is clear that all requests for support of budget, personnel, projects and service programmes *must* be co-ordinated and set in priority by Provinces or Regional Councils. This will involve us in new styles of co-operative partnership with Provinces or Councils, and with each other.

(iii) We affirm these commitments in the conviction that they are consistent with statements of the 1968 Lambeth Conference and the Anglican Consultative Council in 1971 regarding mission. Both affirmed the need for a reappraisal of 'areas of responsibility of the Anglican Communion', and the need for 'joint planning in the light of the total situation' for mission. The joint commitments outlined above are required of us if we are responsibly and mutually to fulfil the mission we share.

The ideas set out in the *aide-memoire* have now been tested in regional consultations in the West Indies and Japan, and in further consultations with the missionary agencies of the churches in Australia, Canada, England, New Zealand, and the USA. Following upon these consultations guidelines for new styles of co-operative partnership are set out in Section B (below).

JOINT CONSULTATION

A *Purpose*

Realizing that the concepts embodied in these proposals are not new, and that much that has been written in recent years about planning for mission through MRI has not yet been translated into action, it is now desired to develop and foster more effective patterns of consultation and working relationships between the member churches of the Anglican Communion. The proposals do not in any way deny the responsibility of each church to determine its own priorities, but are intended to replace former attitudes either of independence or dependence by a common attitude of interdependence. The mutuality involved in the proposed process of joint consultation will enable churches better to appreciate one another's needs and opportunities, as well as one another's responsibilities in relation to the resources entrusted to them.

The proposed process of joint consultation is based on the conviction that both giving and receiving must extend throughout the whole family of Anglican churches, and that every church will receive others as its partners in mission with the variety of resources which they have to offer. Churches which have traditionally been either donors or receivers need to discover the meaning of interdependence, and to examine those areas in which partners can receive from each other. Each church should work towards financial independence in its own structures, but at the same time should be interdependent in the sharing of its spiritual and material resources in the fulfilment of God's mission.

Consultation at the moment is still haphazard and largely unrelated to local planning, and little co-ordination has been attempted between Anglican mission boards and societies. As far as possible, however, existing administrative structures will be utilized in implementing the new patterns of consultation, and the co-ordination of such consultations will be undertaken by the staff of the ACC. The aim is a relation of partnership through mutual consultation, a people-to-people approach as between members of a family of Churches, with a flexibility which corresponds to the varied nature of the member Churches of the Anglican Communion.

The method of circulating projects for support, as exemplified in the

MRI Directory of Projects, easily becomes inflexible, and one of its dangers is that the support is often dependent upon the special interests of the supporting agency. The proposed process of consultation would therefore replace the Directory method, and while attempting to remain faithful to the initial vision of the MRI Directory of Projects, would at the same time, by a more comprehensive and flexible approach, attempt to overcome the defects of this method.

The process of joint consultation will demand from each church that it share with others not only a set of isolated projects, but the context of diocesan and regional mission within which these have meaning and purpose. The data from the consultations will provide an over-view of the total situation of the Anglican Communion. It will be a rich source for study and Communion-wide planning. All parts of the Communion will be able to use the material as the basis for education, communication, and interpretation. The need for resources for the accomplishment of world mission will be able to be more clearly presented, because there will be both more available data, and also greater clarity regarding goals and strategies throughout the Communion.

B Guidelines for Partnership

Thankful for all that the MRI programme has meant to the Anglican Communion in a variety of ways, particularly for introducing the concept of interdependence in our church-to-church relationships, it is now proposed to deepen and develop this interdependence by again emphasizing that:

(a) partnership requires the recognition of the equality of the partners and the discovering of ways in which this equality can be expressed;

(b) all churches have needs which others may help to meet, and resources in which others may share. These needs and resources are not only material but spiritual. Each church should witness to what it has experienced of Christ in its own situation. It will thus provide inspiration and encouragement to other churches; at the same time it should be ready to benefit from their experience.

We therefore recommend the following guidelines:

1. Planning and fixing of priorities should be carried out by each church through its own decision-making process. The basic unit for planning is referred to as a 'church', which will usually be a national church, province, or regional council; but where the situation demands, the basic unit might be smaller or larger.

It is suggested that the process of planning should involve three stages:

(i) the definition of diocesan priorities and objectives;

(ii) the fixing of priorities at the level of the basic unit for planning;

(iii) the sharing of the national, provincial, or regional plan with partner churches through a meeting for joint consultation (partner churches will in some cases exercise their partnership through mission boards or societies). This consultation should at all times preserve the proper freedom of choice of these partners in mission, and also maintain the integrity of the church in each place. The partnership of giving and receiving must also help and not hinder the process by which each church secures its own identity and integrity.

2. Each church should take the initiative in inviting those whom it wishes to be its partners in mission. Partner churches should be invited to participate as consultants in the planning process of a church at an appropriate stage in order to become acquainted with the factors involved in the planning process, to share the experience, and provide the perspective which can be contributed by partners from outside the area. The fact of co-responsibility should also permit the partner churches to raise questions regarding the nature and objectives of the projects proposed.

3. A comprehensive national, provincial or regional plan should be aimed at in stage (ii) of the planning process. This should include the major objectives and programmes of a church (church life, evangelism and community service), and all the resources available and needed for their achievement. The plan should be summarized under a system of categories.

In order to be comprehensive the plan should take into consideration the interrelationships between its various parts, and should include in the planning process every level of the church. Such planning should produce a realistic assessment of the current resources of a church and its needs, human, material, and spiritual, from outside sources.

4. The projects and activities already being carried out or planned by other denominations in the area should also be considered in the planning process. Wherever and whenever possible joint action for mission and the ecumenical sharing of personnel should be undertaken. Any truly comprehensive plan will only be possible if related to the life and work of other denominations, governments, and voluntary agencies.

5. The present procedures of mission boards and societies will need to be modified by the proposed consultative style. Bilateral relationships will be replaced by co-ordinated action.

6. It is considered that three years might be a suitable interval between the meetings for joint consultation. The meetings should take

place in conjunction with meetings already held in a church (e.g. provincial synods), and thus little extra expense would be incurred.

7.   After a three-year comprehensive plan has been developed, in each succeeding year the basic planning groups should review the previous year's activities, the plan as already developed for the two succeeding years, revise or amend it as required, and develop the plan for an additional year. In this way continuity would be achieved for producing the plan to be discussed at the next meeting for joint consultation.

8.   Information regarding the national, provincial, or regional plan of each church will be made available to all other churches.

9.   Emergency needs and needs for special opportunities, which may arise between meetings for joint consultation, should be circulated by the ACC as they arise, through an Emergencies and Opportunities List.

C   *Implementation*

It is proposed that representatives of the churches which have agreed to be partners in mission should meet as outlined in Guideline 6 on the following schedule:

1.   During the first year, August 1973–August 1974: the Church of Uganda, Rwanda, Burundi and Boga Zaire; the Council of the Church of South-East Asia; the Church of the Province of the West Indies; the Nippon Sei Ko Kai; and the Anglican Church of Canada would schedule meetings with their partner churches for the three-year period 1976–79.

2.   During the second year, September 1974–September 1975: meetings would be scheduled for other Churches for the period 1977–80.

3.   During the third year, October 1975–October 1976: meetings would be scheduled for the remaining Churches for the period 1978–81.
   Immediate steps should be taken to develop the schedule for the consultations which would take place in the following member churches: Australia; Brazil; Burma; Central Africa; England; Indian Ocean; Ireland; Kenya; New Zealand; Scotland; South Africa; Sri Lanka (Ceylon); Tanzania; USA; Wales; West Africa; Jerusalem Archbishopric; Anglican Council of South America; South Pacific Anglican Council.

4.   If united Churches (see Limuru Resolution 2) so desire, Anglican Churches are encouraged to maintain or establish relations of partnership with them.

Resolution 27   New Implementation of MRI

The Council:

(a) warmly commends to member churches and missionary agencies the new implementation of the concept of MRI as contained in the Report;

(b) affirms that this implementation will help to break the old pattern of some churches as giving and others as receiving churches, and that it will provide a means by which *all* churches will draw on others for spiritual help and insight, and not merely respond to those who have financial and personal needs;

(c) asks the Secretary General to take appropriate steps towards the implementation of the Programme;

(d) asks the Secretary General, in the interim period and until churches and missionary agencies have accepted and initiated the new proposals, to seek from member churches details of present priorities of uncompleted projects in the 1972/73 Directory, with a view to conveying this information to churches wishing to support projects during this time;

(e) realizing that the proposed planning and consultations may well involve the provision of finance for services to be provided by the ACC Office, and may necessitate an additional staff appointment, agrees that the principle be accepted; and therefore requests, subject to their agreement, that such costs, if they do arise, be shared among the various missionary agencies and boards; and requests the Secretary General to take appropriate action.

Resolution 28   'Membership, Manpower and Money'

The Council receives with appreciation the Report *Membership, Manpower and Money in the Anglican Communion*, commends it to church planning bodies as valuable resource material; asks the Standing Committee to consider and report to ACC 3 the need for a further issue and the form which it should take; and requests the Secretary General to convey to the Reverend Dr David Barrett the Council's gratitude.

5 FINANCE, MEMBERSHIP, AND OTHER MATTERS

A FINANCE

1 STANDING COMMITTEE REPORT

The Council received the following report on finance from the Standing Committee meeting of 14 July 1973:

(a) *Replacement of the ACC Headquarters, London*

As the lease of 21 Chester Street was due to expire in 1975, the Standing Committee, at its meeting in December 1971, instructed the Secretary General to acquire a property to replace it as headquarters of the ACC. The Standing Committee approved the steps that had been taken whereby 32 Eccleston Street, London SW1 has now been acquired.

The Committee expressed sincere thanks to the Episcopal Church in the USA for the generous interest-free loan of $35,000.

The Secretary General reported that the remaining period of the lease of 21 Chester Street had now been sold, and after loans and other charges had been paid off, a small credit balance was anticipated.

(b) *Accounts*

The audited accounts of the Council for the years 1971 and 1972 were received by the Committee on the motion of Mr Cottrell, seconded by the Reverend R. T. Nishimura.

(c) *Provision for ACC 3, Perth, Western Australia, 1975*

Because of the cost of travel to Perth, the Standing Committee was of the opinion that the estimated funds available for the meeting (£36,925) would not be sufficient, and further provision should be made in the budget.

(d) *The Anglican Centre in Rome*

The Committee considered the report on the Anglican Centre in Rome. The gravity of the financial situation was recognized. The Committee was firmly of the opinion that the work and development of the Centre must be enabled to continue, and that in the budget proper provision for this should be made.

(e) *Contribution to the WCC (Limuru Resolution 13)*

The Standing Committee considered that while the use to which the grant was being put was not precisely identical with the original intention, it was closely related and acceptable.

(f) *Inter-Church Conversations*

At Limuru the Council decided that in principle the financing of inter-Church Conversations should be through the ACC budget (Limuru Report, p. 56, no. 5).

60

The Standing Committee in December 1971 recommended that a resolution to implement the principle should be on the agenda for the ACC meeting in 1973.

In confirmation of that recommendation, the Committee agreed to include provision for the inter-Church Conversations in the draft budget.

2 BUDGET FOR 1974 AND 1975

The Council adopted the following Budget and Allocation to the Member Churches:

INTER-ANGLICAN BUDGET 1974 AND 1975

		Proposed Budget 1974 and 1975
Anglican Commitments		
1. *Office of Secretary General	£27,000*	
Contingency Fund	2,540	
2. Meeting of Anglican Consultative Council and Standing Committee[a]	20,000	
3. Jerusalem Archbishopric[b]	2,250	£51,790
Ecumenical Commitments		
1. Anglican Centre in Rome[c]	14,000	
2. World Council of Churches grant[d]	210	
3. Inter-Church Conversations[e]	9,000	£23,210
		£75,000

*Breakdown of budget for the Secretary General's Office:

Salaries	£13,450
Pensions	550
Travel	5,000
Office Expenses	2,500
Office and Housing	5,000
Reserve for Removals	500
	£27,000

a. Includes provision for additional travel costs for 1975 meeting in Perth.
b. The proposal is to phase out this grant. Provision is made for a payment of £2,500 in 1974 and £2,000 in 1975, and thereafter reductions at £500 per annum.
c. Provision is made for a payment of £13,000 in 1974 and £15,000 in 1975.
d. Over two years the allocation covers the final payment of £415.
e. This is a new item in the budget (see above).

ALLOCATION TO THE MEMBER CHURCHES

	1972/73 Percentage	1972/73 Amount	Proposed 1974/75 Percentage	Proposed 1974/75 Amount
Australia	8.50	£4,794	10.00	£7,500
Brazil	.50	282	.50	375
Canada	12.00	6,768	11.00	8,250
Central Africa	.75	423	.75	563
England	30.50	17,202	29.75	22,313
Ireland	1.75	987	1.75	1,312
Japan	.75	423	1.00	750

61

ALLOCATION TO THE MEMBER CHURCHES (*continued*)

	1972/73 Percentage	1972/73 Amount	Proposed 1974/75 Percentage	1974/75 Amount
Jerusalem	.50	282	.50	375
Kenya	.50	282	.75	563
New Zealand	3.00	1.692	3.00	2,250
Scotland	1.50	846	1.50	1,125
South Africa	3.00	1.692	3.00	2,250
Tanzania	.50	282	.75	562
Uganda	.50	282	.75	562
United States of America	30.00	16,920	29.00	21,750
Wales	1.75	987	2.00	1,500
West Africa	1.00	564	1.00	750
West Indies	1.00	564	1.00	750
Extra-Provincial Dioceses including Burma, Indian Ocean (Provinces), Ceylon, and Hong Kong	2.00	1,128	2.00	1,500
		£56,400		£75,000

Breakdown—Extra-Provincial Dioceses

	Budget 1972/73 £	Budget 1974/75 £
Argentina, Paraguay, and Northern Argentina	60	75
Bermuda	120	150
Burma	13	20
Ceylon	—	80
Chile	60	65
Gibraltar	120	150
Hong Kong	185	235
Indian Ocean	180	190
Kuching	60	65
Sabah	60	65
Seoul	60	65
Singapore	90	110
South Pacific Anglican Council	—	100
Taejon	60	65
West Malaysia	60	65
	£1,128	£1,500

Resolution 29   Exchange Rates and Payment of Contributions

When member Churches pay their contributions to the inter-Anglican budget, they should pay whatever sum will provide in £ sterling their allocation as stated in £ sterling in the budget.

3   VOTE OF THANKS

The Council recorded its sincere thanks to the Episcopal Church in the United States of America for a generous interest-free loan of $35,000 to assist in the acquisition of 32 Eccleston Street, London as the new headquarters of the Council.

B   MEMBERSHIP OF THE COUNCIL

1   MINIMUM MEMBERSHIP

Limuru recommended that consideration should be given to reducing the minimum membership for any Province from two members to one (Report, p. 58). The Standing Committee, in December 1971, drafted a schedule of membership on those lines.

The Council in addition took into account the emergence of small Provinces in the Anglican Communion, and new groupings that may be expected, as well as existing patterns as shown in the statistical tables in *Membership, Manpower and Money in the Anglican Communion*.

2   CRITERIA FOR ALLOCATING PLACES IN THE
REVISED SCHEDULE OF MEMBERSHIP

The general but not exclusive criteria used for the revised schedule are based on the 'affiliated membership' (that is, the number of members as given by church records and rolls), as stated in Column 7 of the statistics.

The allocation of places is based on:

Churches with over a million members   3 members each
Other Churches with over a quarter of a million members
                                                        2 members each
Churches with fewer than a quarter of a million members
                                                        1 member each

However, where Provinces join together in some form of regional association and the total affiliated membership exceeds 150,000, such a regional association shall be represented by two members.

3   THE COUNCIL AGREED TO THE FOLLOWING
SCHEDULE OF MEMBERSHIP (Revised 1973)

The membership of the Council shall be as follows:

(*a*) The Archbishop of Canterbury
(*b*) Three from each of the following, consisting of a bishop, a priest or deacon, and a lay person:
     The Church of England in Australia
     The Anglican Church of Canada
     The Church of England

63

The Church of the Province of South Africa

The Church of the Province of Uganda, Rwanda, Burundi, and Boga-Zaire

The Episcopal Church in the United States of America

(c) Two from each of the following, consisting of a bishop, and a priest, deacon, or lay person:

The Church of the Province of Central Africa

The Church of Ireland

The Church of the Province of Kenya

The Church of the Province of New Zealand

The Council of the Church of South East Asia

The Diocese of the Sudan

The Church of the Province of Tanzania

The Church in Wales

The Church of the Province of West Africa

The Church of the Province of the West Indies

(d) One from each of the following, being either a bishop, priest, deacon, or lay person:

Igreja Episcopal do Brasil

The Church of the Province of Burma

The Church of Ceylon

The Church of the Province of the Indian Ocean

The Holy Catholic Church in Japan

The Archbishopric in Jerusalem (except Sudan)

Latin America

The Episcopal Church in Scotland

The South Pacific Anglican Council

(e) One member from each of the following united Churches in full communion with Anglican Churches (Limuru Resolution 2(a)):

The Church of North India

The Church of Pakistan

The Church of South India

(f) Co-opted Members:

The Council shall have power to co-opt up to six additional members, of whom at least two shall be women and two persons not over 28 years of age at the time of appointment.

(g) Additional Members: see 4(b) below.

Note
The present representation of Chung Hua Sheng Kung Hui (China) is through the diocese of Hong Kong in the Council of the Church of South East Asia.

4 TERM OF MEMBERSHIP

(a) Each member is elected for six years except for co-opted members who are nominated for four years.

(b) Extended membership for Chairman and Vice-Chairman. The term of office of the chairman is six years (Constitution 6(b)) which is the same as the term for membership of the Council. As no member is likely to be elected Chairman immediately on appointment to the Council, the Council passed the following:

Resolution 30   Chairman and Vice-Chairman's Term of Appointment
When the Chairman's appointment as Chairman extends beyond the date at which his or her membership of the Council ordinarily expires:
from the time of the expiry of the ordinary membership

(i) the Church he or she represents shall be entitled to elect a new member to succeed him or her as member of Council;
(ii) the Chairman shall become an 'additional member of Council' until the completion of the term as Chairman;
(iii) the same rules shall apply to the Vice-Chairman.

(c) The Council had before it a resolution from Canada that the normal term of membership should be reduced from six to four years. In the interests of continuity in the Council's work, and because a four-year term would involve a change of 50% of the membership for each meeting of the Council, the Council came to the conclusion that the normal term of membership should remain at six years, except for co-opted members.

5   THE LUSITANIAN, OLD CATHOLIC, AND SPANISH REFORMED EPISCOPAL CHURCHES
A recommendation from a meeting in Trier in September 1972 of Anglican, Lusitanian, Old Catholic, and Spanish Reformed Episcopal bishops had been referred to the Council by the Archbishop of Canterbury. The recommendation was:
That Old Catholic and Iberian bishops should be represented on the Anglican Consultative Council.

The Council appreciated the proposal and gave it sympathetic attention. They welcomed the developing collaboration and fellowship between these Churches and the Anglican Church on the continent of Europe.

However, the Council felt that such an invitation to membership of the ACC would need to be further extended to the Philippine Independent Church which is in close co-operation with the Episcopal Church in the Philippines, and to other episcopal Churches with which the Anglican Church is in full communion.

In the case of the united Churches in India and Pakistan, which are already members of the ACC, the Council thought the position was somewhat different, as the united Churches incorporated the former Anglican Churches in those countries.

The Council felt that the ACC, as yet a very young Council, needed more time to find its feet and consider its role before it was ready to take so decisive a step as that proposed in further extending its membership beyond the Anglican Communion.

The Council therefore agreed that the recommendation for Lusitanian, Old Catholic, and Spanish Reformed Episcopal membership of the Council be not proceeded with at the present moment, but that in a few years' time it should be considered again.

6 ADDITIONAL MEMBERS NOT OVER 28 YEARS OF AGE

Resolution 31   Proposal for Additional Younger Members

The Standing Committee is asked to consider amending the Schedule of Membership of the Council to provide for the appointment of an additional two lay persons not over 28 years of age at the time of appointment.

C   OFFICERS OF THE COUNCIL

1   ELECTIONS

The Council elected the following officers. Their term of appointment begins after the meeting of the Standing Committee in 1974, except those signified by * who fill existing vacancies:

Chairman of the Council: Mrs Harold C. Kelleran   USA
Vice-Chairman: Bishop G. C. M. Woodroffe West Indies

To places on the
Standing Committee: Mr J. Bikangaga*   Uganda
                                            Bishop L. W. Brown   England
                                            Archbishop F. Olang   Kenya
                                            Archbishop G. T. Sambell Australia
                                            Archbishop E. W. Scott*   Canada

2   APPOINTMENT OF CHAIRMAN AND VICE-CHAIRMAN

(By clause 6(*b*) of the Constitution of the Council the Chairman and Vice-Chairman are each appointed for six years.)

The Council agreed that clause 6(*b*) be amended to read:

'The Council shall elect a Chairman and Vice-Chairman from its own number, who shall hold office for four years.'

(Note: This resolution requires to be ratified by two-thirds of the Anglican member Churches of the Council before it takes effect.)

3   APPOINTMENT OF SECRETARY GENERAL

Resolution 32   Secretary General

The Standing Committee is empowered to deal with the appointment of the Secretary General should this be necessary at any time between meetings of the Council.

D LEGAL STATUS FOR THE COUNCIL IN THE UNITED KINGDOM

The Secretary General reported exploratory steps that had been taken to determine how the Anglican Consultative Council might attain legal status in the United Kingdom and recognition by the Charity Commissioners for England and Wales. The Council agreed that the matter should be proceeded with, and passed the following resolution, moved by Professor J. N. D. Anderson and seconded by Bishop G. C. M. Woodroffe:

Resolution 33   Legal Status

(i) The Council approves that a Trust be set up in the United Kingdom the object of which shall be to advance the Christian religion in accordance with the terms of the Constitution of the Anglican Consultative Council which may hold on behalf of the Council all property and funds situated in the United Kingdom.

(ii) The Council delegates full responsibility to the Standing Committee to approve on its behalf the final form of the said Trust and to appoint the necessary Trustees.

Carried.   *In favour 47, against nil, abstentions nil.*

E COMMUNICATION IN THE ANGLICAN COMMUNION

1 "CYCLE OF PRAYER" AND "RESPONSE"

The Council received reports on the publications *Cycle of Prayer* and *Response* and gave general approval to the editors' proposals for improvements in future issues. The Council again commended these publications for widespread use in the Anglican Communion.

2 TASK FORCE ON COMMUNICATION

A memorandum introduced by the Presiding Bishop, USA, drew attention to the responsibility of the Anglican Consultative Council under its terms of reference (No. 7) for advising on problems of inter-Anglican communication. The Council passed the following resolution:

Resolution 34   Communication

(a) The Secretary General is authorized to establish a Task Force on Communication which will make recommendations to the Council in 1975 on

(i) the function, use, and distribution of *Compasrose* and *Anglican Information;*

(ii) additional channels for the gathering and dissemination of news from each Church to all the Churches;

(iii) exchange of information regarding available educational and promotional materials;

(iv) encouragement of the use of *Response* and the *Cycle of Prayer;*

(v) the intensification of person-to-person relations among Churches;

(vi) the feasibility of a system of rapid communication such as TELEX.

(*b*) The Task Force on Communication should include persons from the Churches actively involved in these areas of responsibility as well as consultants from the communication field.

F ST GEORGE'S COLLEGE, JERUSALEM

The Archbishop in Jerusalem reported that he had delegated responsibility for the governing of the College to an International Governing Council, made up of representatives of the Church in Jerusalem and the Middle East and including three members appointed by the Standing Committee of the ACC. The International Governing Council will be responsible for all questions of policy, but will be assisted by a Management Committee in Jerusalem.

The Council noted with pleasure the number who had attended courses at the College and that they were representative of several different denominations and many countries of the world.

Resolution 35 St George's College, Jerusalem

The Council

(*a*) receives the report made to it by the Archbishop in Jerusalem that he has delegated to an International Governing Council the joint responsibility for governing the College;

(*b*) commends to the Churches of the Anglican Communion the work of the College and the facilities which it offers as a centre for studies which draw on the unique resources available in the Holy Land.

G CONFERENCE FOR THE ABOLITION OF TORTURE

The Secretary General reported that he had received from Amnesty International an invitation to participate as representing the Anglican Consultative Council in a conference to be held in Paris in December 1973, on 'The Abolition of Torture'. This was to be part of a worldwide campaign for the abolition of torture.

The Council decided that the invitation should be accepted.

H   THE NEXT MEETING OF THE COUNCIL

The Council considered the following recommendation from Section III of the 1968 Lambeth Conference:

World-wide Anglican Congresses should be replaced by *a joint meeting*, at the time of an Assembly of the World Council of Churches, *of the Consultative Council and of Anglican participants in the Assembly* in or near the place where the Assembly is held. This Anglican meeting should receive a report from the Consultative Council on its work and on that of the Secretary General and should consider other matters brought to it by the Council.

(LC Report, p. 145)

The Council considered that if such a gathering were arranged at Perth in 1975 the overall programme might be:

(*a*) WCC Assembly, Djakarta, 20 July–10 August 1975.
(*b*) Joint meeting of ACC and Anglican WCC delegates, Perth.
(*c*) Meeting of the ACC, Perth.

The Council was strongly of the opinion that the joint meeting should be dropped for the reasons that:

(i)   some people would be expected to participate in meetings and travel continuously for about 5½ weeks;
(ii) a worthwhile agenda for the joint meeting, particularly in the wake of the WCC Assembly, would be difficult to contrive;
(iii) much of the value of a congress is that it can provide an encounter with the world-wide Church for people to whom that is a new experience. This would not apply to members of the WCC Assembly and the ACC.

The Council decided that there would be no joint meeting in 1975, and that the sequence of events should be:

(*a*) WCC Assembly, Djakarta, 20 July–10 August 1975.
(*b*) ACC 3, Perth, Western Australia, approximately 13–21 August 1975.

6 REPORT: LITURGY 1968-1973

Limuru Resolution 26 asked that 'a report on liturgical matters be made to the Anglican Consultative Council in 1973'. This report, *Liturgy 1968–1973*, was written for the ACC by Canon Ronald Jasper of Westminster Abbey.

A review of liturgical developments up to 1968 was published in *Preparatory Information* for the 1968 Lambeth Conference, pp. 35–70. Canon Jasper's present report continues the review from 1968.

A Report for the Anglican Consultative Council 1973 by Canon R. C. D. Jasper, D. D.

PART 1: THE STRUCTURE AND CONTENTS OF
THE EUCHARISTIC LITURGY AND THE DAILY
OFFICE
(A Report prepared at the request of the Liturgical Consultation held after the Lambeth Conference, August 1968)

The Lambeth Conference of 1958 passed a Resolution (76) which reads:

> The Conference requests the Archbishop of Canterbury, in co-operation with the Consultative Body, to appoint an Advisory Committee to prepare recommendations for the structure of the Holy Communion service which could be taken into consideration by any Church or Province revising its Eucharistic rite, and which would both conserve the doctrinal balance of the Anglican tradition and take account of present liturgical knowledge.

No action was taken on this Resolution until the Liturgical Consultation held after the Anglican Congress in Toronto in August 1963 when four people (Archbishop Clark, Primate of Canada; Bishop Sansbury of Singapore; Dr Massey Shepherd of the Episcopal Church, USA; and Archbishop Brown of Uganda) were appointed to draw up a document suggesting a basic shape or pattern for eucharistic liturgies. The document was circulated to metropolitans and liturgical consultants in March 1965, but it was not studied or used widely.

The Liturgical Consultation held in London after the Lambeth Conference in August 1968 requested Dr Brown (now Bishop of St Edmundsbury and Ipswich) and Dr Jasper to undertake a revision of the document in the light of the considerable experience of liturgical revision since 1958, in consultation with the other scholars originally concerned. At the same time it was agreed that a similar document should be prepared on the structure of the Daily Office. After due consideration, however, it was thought wise to discuss both questions in a single document. There is nowadays a desire to relate more closely the Daily Office and the Eucharist. Such an arrangement is desirable not only on weekdays, but on Sundays, in those congregations which do not have the Eucharist as their principal act of worship. In many Churches of the Anglican Communion this is the case not from choice, but from necessity, because the number of priests is inadequate. This point is considered in the suggestions made in this document. Sections 1-3 could be used, with little modification, as a Daily Office or a Sunday service without eucharistic celebration: and it could be used either in the morning or in the evening. Experience has already proved this to be a perfectly satisfactory arrangement in a number of places.

Attention should be drawn to the fact that the 1958 Resolution referred specifically to the structure of the Holy Communion service. We have, therefore, concerned ourselves primarily with this aspect in this document: but it is very obvious that the problems of language will also play a large part in the work of liturgical revision for some time to come. There is clearly a desire to use more contemporary forms in all churches, as the work of the International Consultation on English Texts (ICET) indicates. This in itself poses a whole range of new questions, both practical and technical. We believe, however, that the search for contemporary liturgical language should be pursued vigorously; and provided there is a willingness to regard experimental texts as expendable, there is no reason why there should not emerge in the foreseeable future liturgical forms which are truly relevant to the situations in which they are used.

Finally, we wish to emphasize that, although we have considered very carefully the comments and criticisms of the scholars whom we have consulted and have made several amendments to this document in the light of them, we alone bear the responsibility for what is written here.

Leslie St Edmundsbury and Ipswich
Ronald Jasper

The Eucharistic Liturgy and the Daily Office

In the full eucharistic rite we indentify a number of basic elements in the celebration:
1. The Preparation
2. The Ministry of the Word
3. The Prayers
4. The Offertory
5. The Thanksgiving over bread and wine
6. The Breaking of the Bread
7. The Communion
8. The Dismissal

1. *The Preparation*

(a) The celebrant greets the congregation. This greeting could have reference to the season (e.g. at Easter—V. The Lord is risen. R. Alleluia. Indeed he is risen). This greeting should lead into a prayer asking for the help of God the Holy Spirit (e.g. the Collect for Purity or a seasonable collect).

(b) An Act of praise and adoration. The Gloria in Excelsis is very suitable; or a psalm or a hymn (optional on weekdays).

(c) A confession of sins, with absolution or prayer for forgiveness (optional

71

6

on weekdays). Alternatively, this might be placed with the prayers (No. 3) after the Ministry of the Word.

2. *The Ministry of the Word*

(*a*) Scripture Readings, including Psalms. Three lessons should be provided, from the Old Testament, Epistles, and Gospels; although it is likely that in many cases only two of the three readings will be used. These readings can be interspersed with psalms, canticles, or hymns.

(*b*) Sermon (optional on weekdays).

(*c*) Creed—either the Nicene Creed or the Apostles' Creed (optional).

3. *The Prayers*

(*a*) Intercessions with thanksgivings. These may be offered in many forms, A litany form allowing for extemporary prayer and congregational participation is widely appreciated.

(*b*) A confession of sins, with absolution or prayer for forgiveness—if not used in the Preparation (1) (optional on weekdays).

(*c*) The Peace.

These first three elements of the service may be used alone, as one of the Daily Offices: and especially when used on Sundays they may be supplemented with an Act of Thanksgiving and Dedication and the Lord's Prayer before the Pax. In this case the first half of the 1662 Blessing might be regarded as an appropriate form for the Pax. When using these elements as either the Morning or the Evening Office, care should be taken to ensure a systematic use of psalmody and a variety of canticles. Psalmody, canticles, and lessons should be used in both the Daily Offices, although not necessarily in equal proportions; and care should be taken to avoid unnecessary duplication of material.

4. *The Offertory*

A sentence which looks forward to the eucharistic action may be used: but care should be taken not to give any impression that the Offertory is an act of oblation in itself.

5. *The Thanksgiving over bread and wine*

The basic elements and progression of this eucharistic prayer are:

(*a*) Sursum Corda.

(*b*) The proclamation and recital of the mighty acts of God in creation redemption, and sanctification.

(*c*) The Narrative of the Institution.

(*d*) The anamnesis of the work of Christ in Death, Resurrection, and Ascension 'until he come'. It is recognized that this is the most difficult section of the prayer in view of the different doctrinal emphases which are expressed and recognized within the Anglican Communion. The whole concept of anamnesis is, however, so rich in meaning that it should not be impossible to express it in such a way that the needs of everyone are met. Whatever language is adopted should, however, avoid any idea of a propitiatory sacrifice or a repetition of Christ's sacrifice. The 'once for all' character of his work must not be obscured.

(*e*) The prayer that through the sharing of the bread and wine and through the power of the Holy Spirit we may be made one with our Lord and so renewed in the Body of Christ.

The whole prayer is rightly set in the context of praise, e.g. Sursum Corda and Sanctus.

6. *The Breaking of the Bread*

This may be done in silence or may be accompanied by suitable words (e.g. 1 Cor. 10.16–17).

7. *The Communion*

(*a*) The Communion Devotions. These must not be elaborate or distracting from the main action of the liturgy. The basic devotion can be the Lord's Prayer alone, the doxology of which suitably expresses the element of praise at this point.

(*b*) The Communion.

(*c*) The post-communion devotion. This may take the form of a prayer and/or a hymn or canticle of thanksgiving and dedication: but whatever material is used should make the point clear that God's people are to witness and serve as the body of Christ in the world, strengthened by his grace and looking forward to the fulfilment of his promise.

8. *The Dismissal*

It may be found appropriate, as a concession to people's traditional expectation at this point, or for the benefit of non-communicants who are present, to associate a blessing with the actual words of dismissal. It is desirable, however, and certainly logical, that no further devotions should follow the dismissal. This is the final action in the rite.

PART 2: LITURGICAL REVISION IN THE ANGLICAN COMMUNION 1968–1973

Australia, Burma, Canada, Central Africa, Ceylon, England, Ireland, Japan, Jerusalem, Kenya, New Zealand, Scotland, South Africa, Tanzania, United States of America, USA Province IX, Wales, West Africa, West Indies, Extra-Provincial Dioceses. For Latin America see USA Province IX and Extra-Provincial Dioceses.

Australia

In 1969 the Liturgical Commission published *A Service of Holy Communion for Australia 1969*. This was offered for optional use in parishes in which it is authorized by the diocesan bishop following a specific request from the incumbent and people. The service is in contemporary English (including the 'you' form). The text of the Lord's Prayer, Gloria in Excelsis, and the Creed is that of the (then) ICET version. It has had a mixed reception in the Church from people of all traditions. A considerable number of parishes in most of the dioceses have used it and many are still using it. The Liturgical Commission recommends its continued use, alternatively with 1662.

The Commission made available the Collects in contemporary English, together with Old Testament Lections.

English Series 2 has also been recommended by the Liturgical Commission for possible alternative trial use in parishes and it is very popular in some areas. A contemporary English version of it was published by North Queensland but has not come into wide use in other dioceses.

Although all these and other local trial uses (not only of the Eucharist but English Series 2 Baptism and various versions of Morning and Evening Prayer) are proceeding, it is probably true to say that in the majority of parishes in Australia worship generally is still that of the Book of Common Prayer 1662, often with 1928 modifications.

In 1971 the Liturgical Commission published a booklet consisting of a conservatively revised form of Morning and Evening Prayer, The Litany and Holy Communion. The English style generally is close to that of the RSV Bible. This was followed in 1972 by a further booklet, *Sunday Services Revised*, containing the same services in contemporary language, together with a new Order for the Burial of the Dead. The Commission has also adopted, with minor changes, the English two-year Eucharistic Lectionary, and it hopes to have this together with collects generally available in 1973. The use of the English Holy Communion Series 3 has been considered, and it has been decided to leave this to the discretion of each bishop. Two changes have also been decided in the ICET version of the Lord's Prayer: in line 2 'hallowed' was substituted for 'holy', a decision already agreed upon by the churches in the British Isles; and in line 6 the traditional 'lead us not into temptation' was retained.

Burma

The present Prayer Book authorized is the Common Prayer Book of the Church of India, Pakistan, Burma, and Ceylon, revised and printed in 1960. This was translated into the Burmese and Sgaw Karen languages and is now being translated into the Pwo Karen language. Revision of the Prayer Book is envisaged but not in the near future.

Concerning the role of the laity in the church services, Canon S. San Hoo writes:

A training course is given to the laity, which lasts several months each year. Laymen and lay women are beginning to take active parts in the services, preaching, addressing, leading, conducting church services. In some churches, some even take part (assisting) in sacramental services; of course, it is done with the authority of the bishop concerned.

Canada

During the period 1968–72 there have been no authorizations of services to supplement or replace those in the Book of Common Prayer of the Canadian Church. However, a considerable number of liturgies have been used experimentally in dioceses throughout Canada; but none of these has received the imprimatur of the General Synod.

Meanwhile the Doctrine and Worship Committee of General Synod is engaged on a number of projects.

1. Work has proceeded on a new service of Institution and Induction, due for submission to General Synod in May 1973.

2. Work is also proceeding on a new rite of Initiation, and the guide-lines for the subcommittee working on this rite are in line with general trends throughout the Church.

(a) The custom of baptizing infants and young children will, it is assumed, continue. The new rite of baptism will also include the laying on of hands and possibly the administration of Holy Communion.
(b) Children at an early age (7 or 8 years or even younger) will, with the consent of parents, be regular communicants.
(c) What was called Confirmation will be essentially a Renewal of Baptismal Vows. Such a service would not become merely routine, but would require all those participating in it to have some kind of preparation.

3. A subcommittee is gathering non-scriptural material which might be used at special church services as supplementary to scriptural readings.

4. The Canadian House of Bishops requested the Doctrine and Worship Committee to prepare an alternative contemporary eucharistic liturgy to the Book of Common Prayer. There was, however, considerable resistance to this on the part of some committee members, and it was decided that owing to the state of flux prevailing in liturgical affairs, the present was the wrong time to prepare such a liturgy. The existing material was sufficient for the bishops to deal with liturgical matters in their own dioceses.

Central Africa

During the period 1968 to mid-1971 there existed a Liturgical Commission for the Province. To use its own words in its report to Provincial Synod 1969 it did not feel itself 'competent to undertake the major work of Prayer Book revision, which is presently being tackled in other Provinces of the Anglican Communion. It feels that it has neither the liturgical experience, the time nor the opportunity to meet often enough for so great a task. We have, therefore, attempted, over against the provincial need, to review the revisions of others and to decide on what is best and most suitable for this Province's circumstances.' Guided by the Liturgical Commission, Church of England Series 2 Baptism, Confirmation, and Eucharist were all approved for use in the Province, as also were several South African revisions of the Institution of a Priest, the Consecration of a church, the Blessing of a house, and the Admission of Churchwardens and Sidesmen. During this period the Liturgical Commission produced for the Province a revised calendar, to-gether with the principles on which it was drawn up. The 1969 Provincial Synod specifically added three names to the Provincial Calendar—27 January, Leonard Kamungu, Pioneer Priest in Zambia; 17 July, Alston May, Pioneer Bishop in Zambia; 11 October, William Percival Johnson, Pioneer Priest in Malawi. Much work was done on revising the Propers of the Eucharist for Saints' Days according to this calendar. However, this came to an end by mid-1971 since there had come rather an air of unreality about this project because it is obvious that the future lies rather in a rationalized lectionary covering either both Eucharist and Office, as in the present South African and Church of England proposals, or at least Daily Readings throughout the week at the Eucharist, as in the present Roman rite.

By mid-1971 Episcopal Synod had come to the conclusion that needs and resources are so disparate in the Province that it would be better to have national and diocesan liturgical committees rather than one provincial liturgical commission. Consequently the old Liturgical Commission was replaced by a Liturgical Committee for Zambia, a Liturgical Committee for Malawi, a Mashonaland Liturgical Committee, and a Matabeleland Liturgical Committee. The Principal Correspondent for Liturgy for the Province was appointed as the Provincial Liturgical Consultant to combine the various committees together and keep them in touch with Episcopal Synod and Provincial Standing Committee. Mid-1971 saw the publication of a new complete, though shortened, vernacular Prayer Book in the Diocese of Malawi, containing among other things, two eucharistic rites, the first a diocesan version of the provincial liturgy (i.e. the old South African Liturgy with various permissive and up-dating amendments), and the second the 1964 Liturgy for Africa, together with Propers for Sundays and Feast Days based on the South India lectionary. It also contains Baptism and Confirmation based on Church of England Series 2, together with prayers for home, compline, and a selection of psalms with antiphons used as refrains and tunes provided.

Episcopal Synod further authorized for use in the Province Series 2 Morning and Evening Prayer and Churching of Women and the 1968 South African alternative forms of Daily Offices of Morning and Evening Prayer and Holy Communion. Episcopal Synod also authorized the bishops to encourage the experimental use of lectionaries, both for the Eucharist and the Daily Office. In this connection specific approval was given for the use of *Chitsime* (the Roman Catholic eucharistic lections published monthly with commentary in Chichewa, the vernacular language in Malawi), the revised South African lectionary, the South India lectionary, and the lectionary of Series 2.

In Rhodesia an experimental lectionary was produced in 1972 based on the English Series 2 lectionary for weekdays and the South African experimental lectionary for Sundays. This lectionary was intended for use either in the Daily Office alone or in the combined Office and Eucharist. Later, in 1972, the Mashonaland Liturgical Committee produced an improved version of this lectionary for use throughout the whole Province. The Zambia Liturgical Committee has also produced a revised Baptism Series 2 translated into local vernaculars, and new orders for the dedication of a church, the licensing and institution of priests, deaconesses, and lay readers, and the admission of catechumens—all within the context of the Eucharist.

The Episcopal Synod has asked for a form of admission of infants to the catechumenate, for use in cases where heathen parents may wish their children to be raised as Christians, but are not in a position to ask for infant baptism. Finally, there is evidence that in many parts of the Province the use of African liturgical music is developing.

Ceylon

From January 1966 to August 1971 Ceylon followed the Buddhist Poya Week (based on the phases of the moon). This involved most Sundays becoming working days. The Liturgical Commission therefore considered ways in which the Sunday service could be shortened, although it continued to be the main service of the week even when Sunday was a working day. These variations were authorized by the Episcopal Synod of the Church of India, Pakistan, Burma, and Ceylon in January 1970. The most important were as follows:

1. The substitution of a Bible Study with meditation or dialogue for the Ministry of the Word.
2. The omission on certain occasions of the Creed, the Gloria, and the Agnus Dei.
3. The use of certain elements from the Church of England Series 2 rite— the Intercessions, the Prayer of Humble Access, and the Post-Communion Prayers.
4. The use of a shorter Penitential Section.
5. Greater flexibility in the Intercessions.
6. The use of Te Deum, Magnificat, or Benedictus as alternatives to the Gloria.

Certain proposals have also been approved to bring worship more in line with local culture and customs, such as the use of local language, music, dance, ornaments, and architecture. Greater Christian use is also made of days of national significance, e.g. Sinhala and Tamil New Year Day. In religious communities it has been possible to experiment with even greater freedom, e.g. the inclusion of a lesson from the Buddhist Scriptures.

For the future the Liturgical Commission is considering the desirability of a revised daily lectionary and an alternative eucharistic canon.

England

At the beginning of 1968 the work of liturgical reform in the Church of England was already well under way. Two collections of services, First and Second Series, had been published and most of the material in them approved for varying periods of experimental use.

In 1968 the Commission produced *Modern Liturgical Texts*, a collection of modern English translations of some basic liturgical texts including the Lord's Prayer, the Gloria in Excelsis, the Creeds, and Te Deum. With these were anthems with musical (congregational) settings by the Poet Laureate, Cecil Day-Lewis, and the composer Alan Ridout. These were designed as a basis for ecumenical discussion, not for immediate use in any service.

During 1968 the Convocations and House of Laity held long and anxious debates over the Burial Service, chiefly concerned with the propriety of certain formulas in the service for prayer for the departed. The Archbishops received a unanimous report from the representative committee they had appointed to consider the problem, but Convocations rejected most of the recommendations made. The House of Laity then felt unable to approve the service substantially unamended and requested further reconsideration. At the end of 1972 a considerably revised service in modern language was approved by the House of Bishops for presentation in due course to General Synod.

In 1969 the Commission's report *The Calendar and Lessons for the Church's Year* was considered at an informal Liturgical Conference. This incorporated most of the material first presented ecumenically by the Joint Liturgical Group's *The Calendar and Lectionary* but with alterations to suit Anglican needs, e.g. provision for Saints' Days, for Ember Days and special occasions, and to allow more 'floating' sets of lessons for the post-Pentecost or post-Epiphany seasons.There was interest in, and some opposition to, the proposals to start the ecclesiastical year five weeks before Advent; also to the new nomenclature in general (some felt renaming Sundays 'after Pentecost' devalued the doctrine of the Trinity). But the lessons proposed won wide support. Subsequent legal inquiry disclosed difficulties in the way of adopting a new Calendar: for a Calendar could not be authorized under the Prayer Book (Alternative Services) Measure which catered only for services. New legislation would, therefore, be required. In view of much more comprehensive proposals then under consideration by the Church and State Commission it was agreed to defer action on the Calendar in any case.

During the same year the Commission also carried out a nation-wide inquiry on a sample ten per cent of parishes who were at that time already using *Holy Communion, Second Series*. The results confirmed the view that the experimental rite has been widely accepted, and pinpointed certain general criticisms of weak points in that service. These were: the lack of contrition in the confession; the slightly confusing mixture of the elements in the intercession; the lack of seasonal provision; and the inadequacy of the anamnesis section of the Thanksgiving Prayer. (There were also certain formal requests for amendments to be considered from the House of Laity.) The questionnaire also revealed a demand for the use of liturgical silence, and a large minority of clergy and a smaller minority of laity wanted radical revision of the language, away from 'thee' and 'thou'.

In 1970 an international ecumenical body, the International Consultation on English Texts, produced modern English versions of the Lord's Prayer, the Apostles' and Nicene Creeds, the Gloria in Excelsis, Sanctus, Benedictus, and Gloria Patri.* At the same time the Liturgical Commission had begun work on a new Liturgical Psalter; examples of this will be seen in the Burial Service. Thus the desire for modern liturgical material was beginning to be felt and met.

New material was not, however, included in the conservative revision of the Daily Offices which came forward in 1970–71. The main object of *Alternative Services: Second Series (Revised), Morning and Evening Prayer* was to enable Anglicans to use the shorter forms of office proposed in *The Daily Office* which the Joint Liturgical Group published in summer 1968 and which gained great success and popularity. These included not only the greater variety of canticles for weekdays, but also the full two-year weekday lectionary provision, revised and renamed for Anglican use, and the thirteen-week table of psalms. At the same time provision was made by rubric for the use of the daily offices as an alternative form of the Ministry of the Word in the Holy Communion Service. These offices were presented in a long and a shortened form as alternatives, and were approved by the General Synod in February 1971, to take effect superseding Series 2 Morning and Evening Prayer in Advent 1971.

This revision of Second Series material heralded the coming need for a second round of approval or revision for services whose experimental period would shortly expire. It was also realized that the statutory experimental

* *Prayers we have in Common* (G. Chapman 1970), 25p.

period under the Alternative Services Measure would expire within the decade, and that the pace of Synodical work on services must quicken. Series 2 Holy Communion, due to run out in July 1971, had already had to be given a year's extension (granted in Spring 1971) to allow time for the forthcoming 'Series 3' revised rite to appear and be considered by the General Synod. The results of the Commission's questionnaire, the existence of the International (ICET) English texts, and the rising pressure for modern language in liturgical material, were among the many considerations facing the Commission in producing a revision of 'Series 2'. Structurally very little change seemed necessary (though some had asked for penitential material to be put earlier in the service); most other requests were met, including a careful revision of the anamnesis part of the canon. It was agreed to incorporate the ICET texts, and became evident that surrounding material must in this case be in appropriately modern language.

This is the main and most visible change in the rite, entailing not only change from addressing God as 'thou' to 'you' but much consequential syntactical and vocabulary alteration. Much more seasonal material and a new devotion based on the Decalogue were also provided. Appended were the two-year Sunday readings first seen in the Joint Liturgical Group's *Calendar and Lectionary*, plus provision for Saints' Days and special occasions. Work on a new set of collects is still proceeding. Consideration of Series 3 by the General Synod was begun in November 1971 and it was finally authorized for four years' experimental use in November 1972.

In 1971 the Synod also approved temporizing extensions of experimental use for the Baptism and Confirmation services for three more years, and considered (without approving) reports from both the Doctrine and Initiation Commissions whose findings may be relevant to work now being done on these services. In addition to this, the Liturgical Commission is also working on a new Marriage Service (which never appeared in Series 2 form) and on services for the sick.

Ireland

The Church of Ireland Liturgical Advisory Committee is actively engaged in liturgical revision. It reports annually to the General Synod and considers the comments and criticisms made by that body. But the Synod is not asked to give formal sanction to revised services. The bishops issue them for a trial period of up to seven years, provided they are satisfied that revision does not involve a change in doctrine. When the time comes to incorporate a revised service in a Book of Common Prayer a two-thirds majority of both orders in the General Synod is necessary.

The first of the revised services to appear was Holy Communion in 1967. This was followed by Morning and Evening Prayer and Litany and the Baptism of Children in 1969, all of which were published in one booklet. The Offices and the Litany were traditional in style and language: God was addressed as 'thou', but man as 'you'. The Baptism of Children was, however, more radical. In structure it was very similar to the English Series 2 rite, while the language was in 'you' form throughout. It has been very favourably received. Since then work has continued on a revised rite of Holy Communion, and this was published in 1972. Great attention is paid to the structure set out in the document produced at the request of Lambeth Liturgical Consultation of 1968. Work is also going forward on a more contemporary version of the Daily Offices and the Litany. In all these new services it is proposed to incorporate the 'Agreed Texts' proposed by ICET, although the traditional form of the Lord's Prayer will also be permitted. Once the present work is completed it should be possible to envisage a Sunday Service Book in the not too distant future.

Every diocese now has a 'Liturgical Adviser' appointed by the Bishop. These men do valuable work in introducing the new services at parish level, and in gathering local comments and criticisms.

Japan

Nippon Sei Ko Kai has continued to use the revised Prayer Book of 1959. In 1971 the General Synod decided to proceed with a fundamental revision of the Prayer Book in colloquial Japanese, and a Prayer Book Revision Committee was appointed by the House of Bishops. An unofficial translation into English of the Communion Rite from the 1959 Revised Prayer Book was also published in 1971 under the title *The Eucharistic Liturgy*. Two translations are given—one in traditional liturgical English and one in modern English.

Jerusalem Archbishopric

In Iran no major liturgical developments have taken place: but the revision of different services is contemplated, mainly based on the new revisions appearing in England. The revised calendar and lectionary proposed by the Church of England Liturgical Commission in 1968 is being followed. The new collects have also been translated into Persian and are now being used experimentally for a period of one or two years.

Kenya

When the new Province was inaugurated in 1970 the use of the liturgical books authorized in the former Province of East Africa continued. In June 1972 the Theological and Liturgical Panel met for the first time. It decided:

1. that no full liturgical revision could be undertaken until African liturgical scholars were available;
2. that a revision of the language of some of the services from the 1662 Book was urgently necessary, especially for use in schools and in towns where young people liked to attend English services.

The Panel had before it four documents:

(*a*) *Morning and Evening Prayer in Modern English* published by the Central Tanganyika Press by arrangement with the Church Pastoral Aid Society.
(*b*) *An Experimental Service in English for use at Morning Prayer*, St Stephen's Pro-Cathedral, Kisumu.
(*c*) *Service of Holy Communion*, Kisumu Parish (experimental), 2nd draft.
(*d*) *Baptism of Children* (Draft Service in Modern English).

The Panel decided that if the bishops agreed, a fresh draft of Morning and Evening Prayer and of Holy Communion would be prepared by two of its members for submission to a working party to be called early in 1973.

It also recommended the continued use of the United Liturgy for East Africa, but not the Liturgy for Africa, since the use of too many experimental liturgies only made for confusion.

New Zealand

In 1970 the General Synod authorized for general use as an alternative to the eucharistic rites of 1662 and 1928 *The New Zealand Liturgy 1970*. The basic structure is the same as that of the experimental liturgy of 1966, and the language is in a contemporary style. There are, however, two important changes made in the light of a resolution of General Synod in 1968:

(a) The texts of the Gloria, Nicene Creed, and Lord's Prayer are those agreed upon by ICET.
(b) Seasonal proper prefaces have been added to the Eucharistic Prayer.

This rite is now being translated into Maori.

The General Synod also authorized in 1970 the revised orders of Baptism and Confirmation entitled *Christian Initiation 1970*. Here, although the baptism of infants with confirmation at a later age is accepted, the principal rite is an integrated one of baptism, laying on of hands, and first communion for adults.

The Prayer Book Commission is also making use of Diocesan Prayer Book Committees to do experimental work in different fields.

In 1972 the General Synod authorized the following services:

1. The New Zealand Liturgy 1970 as an alternative to 1662 and 1928.
2. The continued use of Christian Initiation 1970 and Alternative Sunday and Daily Services 1968 for two years.
3. The Funeral Service 1972 for two years. This contains alternative forms of commendation, prayers for special occasions, and a service for the disposal of ashes.
4. The Marriage Service 1972 and an alternative Calendar for two years.

Work is also proceeding on material for the Ministry to the Sick and a service of Thanksgiving after Childbirth.

Scotland

In 1970 a further revision of the experimental eucharistic liturgy of 1966 was produced. The language of this rite is traditional. A proposal to modernize the language of the Canon was submitted to the Provincial Synod; but it received little encouragement. Authorization has also been given for the use of the eucharistic lectionaries of the Roman Catholic Church and the Joint Liturgical Group.

Agreement has been reached with the Roman Catholic Church on the texts of a Preamble and a Prayer for use in the baptismal rites of both Churches; but these still await authorization. Work is also proceeding on a revision of the following: the Daily Offices, the Visitation and Communion of the Sick, and the Institution of a Rector.

South Africa

The Liturgical Committee of the Church of the Province of South Africa published in 1969 Proposed Alternative Forms of the Daily Office and Holy

81

Communion. These have been authorized for experimental use by the Synod of Bishops until the 21st Sunday after Penetecost 1973.

The Calendar and Lectionary are based on that produced by the Joint Liturgical Group in England and edited by Canon R. C. D. Jasper.

A Form of Morning Prayer is provided, designed to be used either as the synaxis before Holy Communion or independently in place of the Prayer Book form of Morning Prayer (or Evening Prayer if Holy Communion is held in the evening).

The Holy Communion is based on the Second Series authorized in the Church of England in 1967.

A second office is provided for use instead of Evening Prayer, or instead of Morning Prayer if Holy Communion is in the evening.

A set of 'Modern Collects' for use with the Alternative Forms was also produced in 1972. It is not intended to provide merely a modern translation of the original collects taken from the Latin. Nor has it been the plan merely to change the form of English from the Elizabethan to a contemporary style. The aim is to produce a set of collects appropriate to the liturgy and lectionary provided in the Alternative Forms.

Tanzania

Since 1968 there have been no major liturgical developments in the Province. At the time of its formation in 1970 the liturgical books authorized in the Province of East Africa were taken as authorized.

In 1968 a new translation of the Book of Common Prayer was published for use in the ex-CMS dioceses; and in 1971 the liturgical panel of the new Province began the process of compiling a Provincial liturgy. Consultations are also taking place ecumenically with the Church of Rome with regard to agreed translations of the Lord's Prayer and other common forms.

At the Provincial Synod in August 1972 a draft Liturgy, based on the United Liturgy for East Africa, was discussed and approval was given for its use.

United States of America

The Standing Liturgical Commission of the Protestant Episcopal Church continued to collect from large numbers of clergy and laity their reactions to the eucharistic liturgy approved for experimental use for a period of three years by the General Convention of 1967. At the same time work proceeded on other services. As a result a comprehensive set of revised rites was published in 1970 in *Prayer Book Studies 18–24* and these were authorized for experimental use by the General Convention in the same year. In 1971 they were published in a single volume *Services for Trial Use*, generally known as 'The Green Book'. The new rites are a noteworthy achievement: they contain forms in contemporary language, they include the common texts proposed by ICET, and they have much more variety and flexibility than their predecessors. The main features of the proposals are as follows:

(a) Holy Baptism with the Laying on of hands (P. B. Studies 18). Here there is a return to primitive Christian practice by combining baptism, confirmation, and first communion in one integrated rite, which will be the norm, even for children.

(b) The Church Year (P.B. Studies 19). The Calendar of Feasts and Fasts is that of 1967 with certain modifications. The primacy of Sunday is emphasized; octaves are eliminated; seven new Red Letter days are included; the season of pre-Lent disappears; and Sundays after Trinity become Sundays after Pentecost. All collects are in 'thou' and 'you' forms. The lectionary is the new three-year lectionary of the Roman Catholic Church with certain adjustments.

(c) The Ordination of Bishops, Priests, and Deacons (P.B. Studies 20). The rites are simpler, and clearer in their expression of the functions of the various orders. The ordination prayer for bishops is a free translation of the ancient Hippolytean prayer, while the ordination prayers for priests and deacons are indebted to the South Indian and the proposed Anglican–Methodist rites.

(d) The Holy Eucharist (P.B. Studies 21). The 1966 rite was important in following the basic structure of the early liturgies. Reaction to it has been generally favourable, and so the pattern has been retained. Three rites have been provided. The first is in traditional language, following the 1966 rite with additional variety provided by seven alternative prayers of intercession, an alternative shortened canon, and provision for optional omissions. The second is in contemporary language, also with seven alternative prayers of intercession and an alternative canon. The third is simply an outline together with the texts of four alternative canons; this is intended for informal, special occasions, and the outline is filled in with material to suit the particular occasion.

(e) The Daily Office (P.B. Studies 22). Two forms of the Daily Office are provided, one in traditional and one in contemporary language. There are also midday and evening prayers and daily devotions. Variety and flexibility are produced in the offices by the provision of additional canticles, alternative sets of versicles and responses, and the permission to omit one canticle and one lesson in each office. The offices may also be used as an alternative form of the Ministry of the Word at Holy Communion.

(f) The Psalter. Part 1 (P.B. Studies 23). A fresh translation in contemporary language of seventy-one of the most frequently used psalms. This is the first instalment of a fresh translation of the entire Psalter.

(g) Pastoral Offices (P.B. Studies 24). These include revised forms of the rites of Marriage, Thanksgiving after Childbirth, the Ministry to the Sick, and Burial.

There also appeared in 1970 *A Short Book of Common Prayer in the Common Speech of Today*. This project was undertaken at the request of the Missionary District of Alaska for use there and in other parts of the Church where the linguistic needs of the congregations make simple language necessary. It is 'recommended for use in special situations when authorized by the Bishop'. In spite of this massive provision of new material, there are several projects still to be completed, notably a lectionary for the Daily Office, the translation of the remainder of the Psalter, a Catechism, new alternatives to the forms for the Consecration of churches and the Institution of Ministers, and a collection of Prayers, Thanksgivings, and Litanies.

In 1971, in Province IX of the Episcopal Church (the countries of Central America and the Spanish-speaking Caribbean), *La Santa Eucaristia* was published, containing the full Spanish text for congregational use of three experimental eucharistic rites together with the Propers for Sundays, Saints' Days, and Special Occasions.

Wales

In 1969, the Governing Body authorized for experimental use new orders for Morning and Evening Prayer, with the Litany and a new Lectionary. The structure of the Offices is not very different from that of the 1662 Prayer Book. There is a new penitential introduction, provision is made for a sermon either after the second lesson, the third collect, or the Intercessions, some Intercessions are provided, and it is permitted to finish the Office after the Apostles' Creed when the Litany is to follow immediately, and to omit everything after the second lesson at Morning Prayer and after the Nunc Dimittis at Evening Prayer when the Holy Eucharist is to follow immediately.

The new Lectionary arranges the recitation of the Psalter on a ten-weekly basis, the psalms on Saturday night being suitable in preparation for Sunday worship, and those on Monday morning (mainly sections of Ps. 119), as an introduction to the week's Daily Offices. The weekday Bible readings are on a *Lectio Continua* basis, while the Sunday ones are on certain themes. The Sunday themes are set out in a booklet produced by the Standing Liturgical Commission and published in 1970, called *Introducing Sunday Lessons*.

Also during 1969, the Standing Liturgical Commission published *A Guide to the Parish Eucharist*. This book was intended to help the clergy with the celebration of the experimental Eucharist (which came into use on Low Sunday, 1967).

1970 saw the authorization for use of the forms of Baptism and Confirmation which should appear in the Prayer Book. It is assumed that Baptism will normally take place during Sunday worship, but a 'Ministry of the Word' is provided for use when Baptism is administered separately. The Creed (whether in the 'Ministry of the Word', Morning and Evening Prayer, or the Eucharist), is said by all, and is not repeated in interrogatory form before the Baptism, where it is replaced by a question based on the summary of the Creed in the old Prayer Book Catechism. The Baptism is followed by the signing with the cross and two optional ceremonies, the clothing in a white vesture and the giving of a lighted candle.

Since the 'BCP' forms of Baptism and Confirmation came into use, the Governing Body has received (in September 1971) a report entitled *Christian Initiation* from the Doctrinal Commission of the Church in Wales. At this stage, the report has only been commended for study in parishes, and no action has been taken. If action is taken on it, the Baptism and Confirmation rites of 1970 are likely to have to be revised for an unexpected third time, since the Doctrinal Commission recommends that 'the baptismal act should be followed by an imposition of the hand or consignation, with accompanying words expressive particularly of the gift of the indwelling Spirit through baptism'. The effect of the report's recommendations would appear to be to render Confirmation as a separate rite obsolete. The report also calls for a service of thanksgiving and blessing as an alternative to Baptism for those parents who desire it. This suggests that the old order for Churching may have to be resuscitated and adapted.

In September 1970, the Governing Body authorized the experimental use of the Ministry to the Sick. This provision contains an office for the sick, acts of faith and repentance and auricular Confession, Laying on of Hands, Unction, Holy Communion (either with a celebration of the Eucharist in the sick person's house or from the reserved Sacrament), prayers of commendation at a death-bed, and a number of prayers, Bible readings, and a Litany for the devotional use of the sick person. It is hoped to publish soon a *Companion to the Ministry to the Sick*, containing Christian teaching on sickness, instructions about the various ministrations to help the sick person and his family, and notes on how to conduct the ministrations for the priest.

In March 1971, the Standing Liturgical Commission published a little book called *Services and Ceremonies*. This book contains provision for the Presentation of our Lord, Ash Wednesday, Holy Week, and Easter. Most of the traditional ceremonies are included in it. This publication is an unofficial one and its contents do not form part of the official liturgy of the Church in Wales. However, the Bishops have permitted its use and it has already proved quite popular.

The Standing Liturgical Commission hopes to publish soon a modern English version of the experimental Eucharist. This will be for study purposes only at this stage.

The Standing Liturgical Commission has been represented on the Joint Liturgical Group of the Council of Churches for Wales, which has recently published a small symposium, *Thine is the Glory*, which contains contributions from members of most of the chief Christian traditions in Wales.

The preparation of the Calendar in its 'BCP' form is about to begin. By a happy coincidence, the two Roman Catholic dioceses in Wales (Menevia and Cardiff) are also engaged in calendar revision at the same time and representatives of the two Communions have agreed to try to reach a common mind on which of the Welsh Saints to include in their calendars and the dates upon which to commemorate them.

West Africa

In the dioceses of Sierra Leone and Accra there is an increasing use of the English Series 2 liturgy; but Northern Nigeria still largely maintains the use of 1662. A committee is to study the possibility of creating a liturgy for the Province of West Africa.

The West Indies

In December 1970, the Liturgical Committee was asked to consider proposals for the revision of the West Indian experimental liturgies of 1951 and to produce a draft of a revised liturgy. This proposed draft was submitted to the General Synod of the Province in June 1972.

As a result the Synod agreed that further experimentation and study was needed before a new liturgy for the Province could be agreed upon. It was, therefore, resolved that a Provincial Liturgical Commission should be established, to be assisted by liturgical committees in each diocese, where experiment should be permitted in order to allow indigenous material to emerge.

Extra-Provincial Dioceses

(a) *North and Central Europe and Gibraltar*

In the jurisdiction of North and Central Europe and in the diocese of Gibraltar, the liturgies in use are those currently authorized for the Church of England in the Provinces of Canterbury and York. The Series 2 rite of Holy Communion is used quite widely in the chaplaincies of the jurisdiction of North and Central Europe; but in Gibraltar its adoption is going rather more slowly.

(b) *Mauritius*

An Order for Holy Communion has been produced and authorized for interim use in the diocese. It is available in both English and French.

(c) *South America—Chile, Bolivia, and Peru*

Two liturgical groups have been at work within the diocese, one covering the Santiago–Valparaiso area and the other in the Cautin–Malleco region in South Chile. They work independently but submit their work for discussion and comment to each other; and, pressed by the need to provide services, have in fact produced quite a volume of liturgical material. Their work includes Sunday Worship, Baptism, Holy Communion, Confirmation, Holy Matrimony, etc., and has been produced in a loose-leaf book under the title *Anglican Services of Worship* (*Cultos Anglicanos*). These services have been produced in Spanish.

7 OUR STAY IN IRELAND

Ireland of the Thousand Welcomes they call it, and throughout our stay Ireland lived up to its name in the unique Irish way, welcoming us officially, semi-officially, and by the good manners of its friendly citizens, always glad to offer help to lost Anglicans. What other country calls its tourist organization 'The Board of Welcome'?

Our stay provided many anomalies that break down the easy stereotypes of headline-acquired 'knowledge'. We were housed in the almost-new Church of Ireland Training College, built by the Government for the Church as a training and demonstration-school centre. Its attractive campus and fine buildings were admirable for our labours, and its staff zealous to provide for all our needs. The newly elected President of the Republic is an Anglican, who joined us at Christ Church Cathedral as well as at the Church of Ireland reception for the Council. A memorable vignette of the Government Reception in the State Apartments of Dublin Castle was a glimpse, across one of the lovely Georgian rooms, of Cardinal Conway in deep conversation with the Archbishop of Canterbury.

We are fifty-nine people, from thirty-four nations, five continents, and the islands of many seas. Every race was represented, the thirty-four Caucasians outnumbered non-Caucasians. We are of all orders of ministry, with archbishops and bishops almost equal in number to the clergy and laity. Our average age would be in the fifties, but our two under-twenty-eights contributed much to our thought and life. All of us speak English, in varied accents, whether it is our first or second language. All of us share some sense of the world as Global Village.

Our Anglicanism was symbolized in our President, the Archbishop of Canterbury, who convened us and sat through our very long plenary sessions and participated in each of our section meetings. His observations were wise and definite, always exactly on target, and in every aspect of our life he took full part.

We are representative in only a limited sense, but we reflect our people at home. We have come to know each other more deeply, and care more personally, and have tried genuinely to enter into the concerns of our Churches on the other side of everyone's world. In a word, we are growing.

Thank you, Ireland, for your welcomes, your life shared with us, your special gifts so hard at work on all your problems. We pray for your peace, which is ours too.

MARION KELLERAN

OFFICERS OF THE COUNCIL, DUBLIN 1973

PRESIDENT

The Archbishop of Canterbury

CHAIRMAN

Sir Louis Mbanefo (West Africa)

VICE-CHAIRMAN

Mrs Harold C. Kelleran (USA)

STANDING COMMITTEE

The Chairman and Vice-Chairman of the Council
The Venerable E. D. Cameron (Australia)
The Most Reverend R. S. Dean (Canada)
Professor J. N. D. Anderson (England)
The Reverend R. T. Nishimura (Japan)
Mr J. C. Cottrell (New Zealand)
The Right Reverend G. C. M. Woodroffe (West Indies)

SECRETARY GENERAL

The Right Reverend J. W. A. Howe
32 Eccleston Street, London SW1W 9PY, England

Note
For new Officers of the Council see p. 66 above.

THE SECOND ANGLICAN
CONSULTATIVE COUNCIL

NAMES OF MEMBERS
The Section to which a member belonged is indicated in brackets

		TERM OF OFFICE ENDS*
PRESIDENT	The Most Reverend Michael Ramsey Archbishop of Canterbury	*ex-officio*
AUSTRALIA	The Most Reverend G. T. Sambell Archbishop of Perth (2)	1975
	The Venerable E. D. Cameron (1)	1974
	Mr R. T. St John (3)	1973
BURMA	The Most Reverend J. Aung Hla Archbishop of Burma (*absent*)	1977
	Daw Katherine Khin Khin (*absent*)	1975
	The Right Reverend V. G. Shearburn (*alternate*) (4)	
CANADA	The Most Reverend R. S. Dean Archbishop of Cariboo (3)	1976
	The Venerable L. F. Hatfield (2)	1973
	Miss Betty C. Graham (*Secretary* 4)	1977
CENTRAL AFRICA	The Right Reverend J. P. Burrough Bishop of Mashonaland (1)	1975
	The Reverend J. Malewezi (2)	1973
ENGLAND	The Right Reverend L. W. Brown Bishop of St Edmundsbury and Ipswich (1)	1975
	The Reverend P. H. Boulton (2)	1973
	Professor J. N. D. Anderson (3)	1974
INDIAN OCEAN	The Most Reverend E. E. Curtis Archbishop of the Indian Ocean (3)	1979
	Mr M. Rakotovao (2)	1979
IRELAND	The Right Reverend J. W. Armstrong Bishop of Cashel and Emly, Waterford and Lismore (*Secretary* 3)	1973
	Mr D. W. Bleakley (*Chairman* 2)	1977

*After meeting of Council or Standing Committee in that year.

		TERM OF OFFICE ENDS*
JAPAN	The Right Reverend J. M. Watanabe Bishop of Hokkaido (2)	1973
	The Reverend R. T. Nishimura (4)	1976
JERUSALEM	The Most Reverend G. Appleton Archbishop in Jerusalem (4)	1975
	The Reverend S. Kafity (1)	1977
KENYA	The Most Reverend F. H. Olang Archbishop of Kenya (4)	1975
	The Venerable S. Magua (1)	1973
LATIN AMERICA	The Most Reverend A. R. Kratz Primate of Brazil (4)	1977
	The Reverend Sergio Carranza (*Secretary* 3)	1973
NEW ZEALAND	The Most Reverend A. H. Johnston Archbishop of New Zealand (1)	1977
	Mr J. C. Cottrell (4)	1976
SCOTLAND	The Most Reverend F. H. Moncreiff Primus (1)	1975
	The Very Reverend A. E. Hodgkinson (4)	1977
SOUTH AFRICA	The Right Reverend B. B. Burnett Bishop of Grahamstown (*Secretary* 1)	1977
	Mr Michael R. Rantho (4)	1975
SOUTH-EAST ASIA	The Right Reverend J. Pong Bishop of Taiwan (3)	1973
	The Reverend F. S. Yip (2)	1975
SOUTH PACIFIC	The Right Reverend J. W. Chisholm Bishop of Melanesia (2)	1975
	The Venerable Jabez Bryce (*Secretary* 4)	1977
SRI LANKA (CEYLON)	The Right Reverend C. L. Wickremesinghe Bishop of Kurunagala (*Secretary* 2)	1973
	Mr T. R. Navaratnam (1)	1975
TANZANIA	The Right Reverend M. L. Wiggins Bishop of Victoria Nyanza (4)	1977
	The Reverend M. K. Mbwana (*Secretary* 1)	1973
UGANDA, RWANDA, BURUNDI, AND BOGA-ZAIRE	The Right Reverend J. Luwum Bishop of Northern Uganda (1)	1973
	Mr J. Bikangaga (3)	1977

		TERM OF OFFICE ENDS*
UNITED STATES OF AMERICA	The Right Reverend J. E. Hines Presiding Bishop (1)	1973
	The Reverend W. G. Henson Jacobs (2)	1973
	Mrs Harold C. Kelleran (3)	1976
WALES	The Most Reverend G. O. Williams Archbishop of Wales (*Chairman* 1)	1973
	Mr J. C. P. de Winton (*absent*)	1975
WEST AFRICA	The Most Reverend M. N. C. O. Scott Archbishop of West Africa (*Chairman* 4)	1975
	Sir Louis Mbanefo (3)	1974
WEST INDIES	The Right Reverend G. C. M. Woodroffe Bishop of the Windward Islands (*Chairman* 3)	1979
	The Reverend W. E. Thompson (*Secretary* 2)	1977
CO-OPTED	The Right Reverend J. W. H. Flagg (South America) (2)	1977
	Professor Chin Man Kim (Korea) (3)	1977
CO-OPTED (WOMEN)	Mrs N B King'ori (Kenya) (3)	1975
	Miss Irene F. Jeffreys (Australia) (1)	1975
CO-OPTED (UNDER 28)	The Reverend R. Phillip (South Africa) (2)	1975
	Miss Lindsay M. A. Smith (England) (4)	1977
UNITED CHURCHES	The Right Reverend R. S. Bhandare Bishop of Nagpur, Church of North India (4)	
	The Right Reverend Inayat Masih Bishop of Lahore, and Moderator, Church of Pakistan (2)	
	The Right Reverend A. R. Samuel Bishop of Krishna-Godavari, and Acting Moderator, Church of South India (1)	

IN ATTENDANCE

CONSULTANTS	The Reverend Dr E. R. Fairweather, Trinity College, Toronto, Canada The Reverend U. T. Holmes, University of the South, Sewanee, USA The Reverend J. L. Houlden, Cuddesdon College, Oxford, England The Very Reverend Dr E. W. Kemp, Dean of Worcester, England

The Right Reverend P. A. Reeves, Bishop of Waiapu, New Zealand

The Reverend Canon H. A. E. Sawyerr, Principal and Professor of Theology, Fourah Bay College, University of Sierra Leone

The Right Reverend B. N. Y. Vaughan, Dean of Bangor, Wales

OBSERVERS

The Reverend Professor J. M. Barkley, Irish Council of Churches

The Reverend R. A. Nelson, Irish Council of Churches (*alternate*)

The Reverend Canon W. A. Purdy, Vatican Secretariat for Promoting Christian Unity

The Reverend Dr W. Simpfendörfer, World Council of Churches

The Reverend Dr W. Stewart, British Council of Churches

STAFF

The Right Reverend J. W. A. Howe (Secretary General)

The Reverend F. D. Chaplin (Secretary General's Staff, and Editorial Committee)

Miss Pamela Bird (Secretary General's Staff)

Miss Josephine M. A. Walker (Secretary General's Staff)

Colonel R. J. A. Hornby (Secretary General's Staff—Press and Publicity Consultant)

The Reverend T. M. Anthony (Church House, Toronto; Editorial Committee)

Mrs D. R. Hunter (Executive Council, New York; Editorial Committee)

The Reverend Fr R. A. Masters, S.S.M. (Board for Mission and Unity, London; Editorial Committee)

The Reverend Michael Moore (Archbishop's Counsellors on Foreign Relations, Lambeth)

Miss June Inman (Archbishop's Counsellors on Foreign Relations, Lambeth)

INDEX